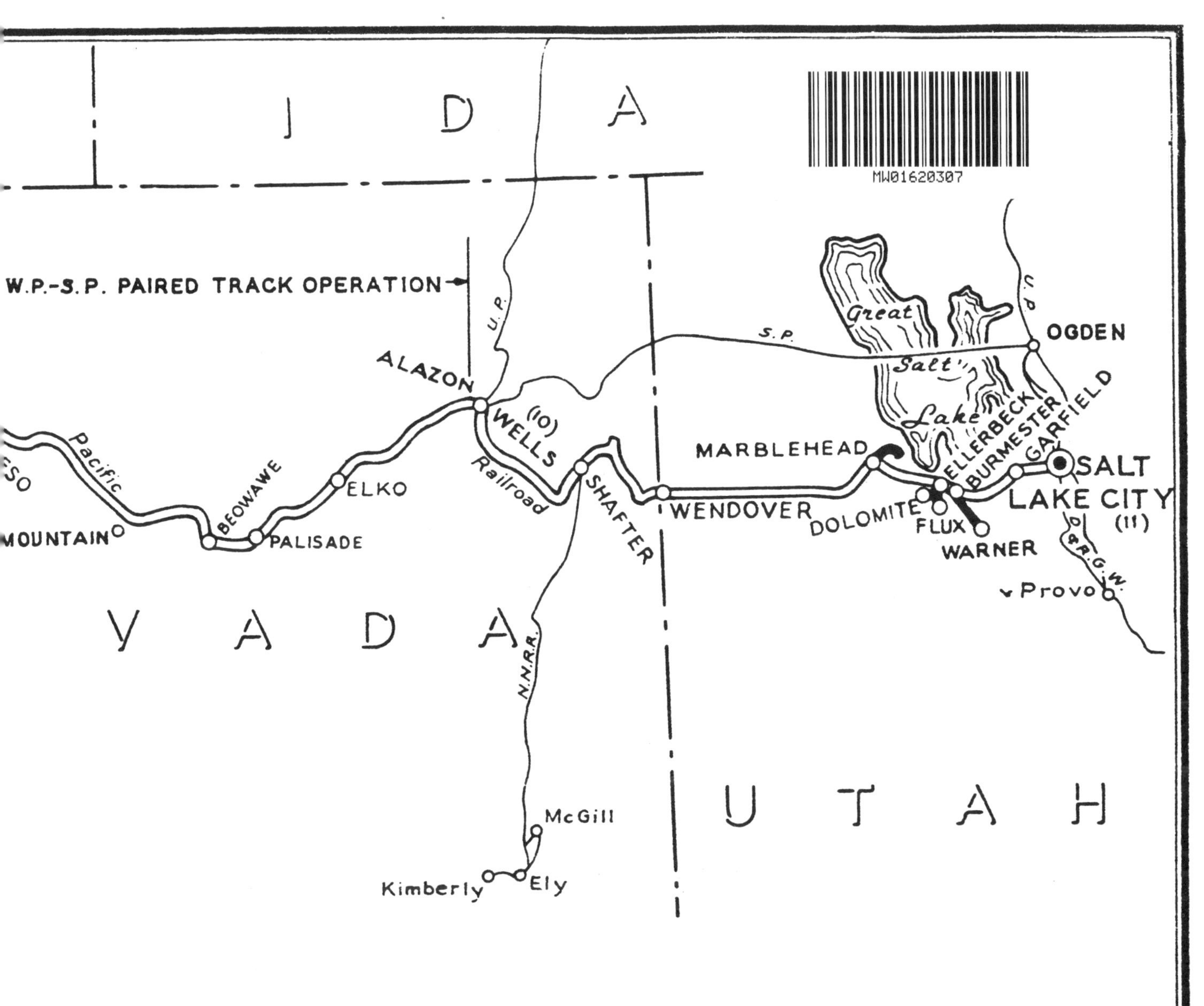

THE WESTERN PACIFIC RAILROAD COMPANY
SYSTEM

k or

Branches

Scale in Miles

0 10 20 30 40 50 60 70 80 90 100

Western Pacific Locomotives and Cars

Steam • Diesel • Passenger • Freight

by Patrick C. Dorin

TLC PUBLISHING INC.

1998
TLC Publishing, Inc.
1387 Winding Creek Lane
Lynchburg, Virginia, 24503-3776

Dedicated to Dr. Fred Beier
Professor of Transportation, University of Minnesota.
Longtime friend of the author
and former employee of the Western Pacific.

The cover painting by noted railroad artist Andrew Harmantas was commissioned specially for this book. It captures a typical scene in California's Feather River Canyon during Western Pacific's transition from steam to diesel.

International Standard Book Number 1-883089-34-4
Library of Congress Catalog Card Number 97-62134

Design, Layout, Type and Image Assembly by
Kevin J. Holland
Type&Design Associates
Burlington, Ontario

Color Image Assembly, Separations and Printing by
Walsworth Publishing Company
Marceline, Missouri, 64658

Produced on the MacOS™

Acknowledgments

I would like to thank the following people for their kind assistance with this look at the Western Pacific Railroad's motive power and rolling stock:

Tom Dixon of TLC Publishing encouraged this project and guided the final contents of the book, which was designed by Kevin J. Holland. My wife Karen offered kind assistance with proofreading and provided constructive input.

Many people provided a tremendous amount of information, mechanical data and photographs, including John Ryzckowski, Bob Larson and George R. Cockle. From the Western Pacific and Union Pacific Railroads, R.E. Shideler (Assistant Superintendent Car Department), John K. Kelly (Director of Public Relations) and Bernard E. Pederson (Director of Advertising and Public Relations, Western Pacific Railroad). Luther Miller of *Railway Age* Magazine, Dr. Fred Beier (University of Minnesota), Dr. Dan Jacobson (Michigan State University), Harold K. Vollrath, Bob Lorenz, Thomas A. Dorin, Michael A. Dorin, Bob Blomquist, J.R. Quinn, Jim Shaw, Howard W. Ameling, Peter Arnold and Chuck Yungkurth (Rail Data Services) also offered valuable assistance.

To all, a huge thank you. Without your kind assistance, this book simply would not have been possible. Should an acknowledgement have been inadvertently omitted here, I trust that it will be found in the appropriate location within the text.

Table of Contents

(TLC Collection)

Introduction

The purpose of this book is to provide a review of Western Pacific motive power and rolling stock. A brief text introduces each chapter, followed by a series of photographs, equipment rosters and diagrams. It is hoped that the material will give model railroaders a reference text for their equipment construction projects, and that it will bring back fond memories of the Western Pacific and the types of equipment that were needed to fulfill the needs of the shipping and traveling public.

The Western Pacific was a unique transportation company with high levels of maintenance and positive employee and customer relations. Although the company is no longer a separate organization, but part of the Union Pacific System, we could say that the WP lives on not only in the hearts and minds of many railroad enthusiasts but also through the fact that WP reporting marks still grace newly repainted rolling stock of the Union Pacific.

As a final comment, and I am not sure how many would agree with this statement, but wouldn't it be nice if the Union Pacific System kept at least one or two operating locomotives in the original Western Pacific scheme as well as one or two in the UP scheme with WP lettering?

Patrick C. Dorin
Superior, Wisconsin
October 17, 1997.

1 Steam Locomotives

Construction of the Western Pacific began in 1906. At that time, the railroad owned no locomotives of its own, but borrowed five locomotives from the Denver & Rio Grande and six from the Rio Grande Western. At the same time, the company ordered twenty 2-8-0s from the Baldwin Locomotive Works at Philadelphia. These locomotives were numbered, naturally, from 1 to 20. The company had also purchased two 4-6-0 freight locomotives from the Alameda & San Joaquin, which were numbered 121 and 122. Until 1908, these locomotives were all the Western Pacific either owned or operated. (1)

Western Pacific received its first passenger power in 1908 as construction of the railroad neared completion. This involved an order for 15 passenger 4-6-0s from Alco's Brooks Works in Dunkirk, New York. In 1909, two very large orders were placed with the American Locomotive Company. This group included 45 2-8-0s for freight service, numbered 21 to 65. These engines were similar to the Baldwin 2-8-0s ordered in 1906. Twenty more passenger 4-6-0s were purchased from Alco, boosting the grand total of passenger power to 36 locomotives, numbered 71 to 106.

The second 1909 order went to Alco's Pittsburgh Works for a dozen 0-6-0 switch engines with slope back tenders. The WP was now ready to begin full service to the shipping and traveling public. The roster would remain relatively stable over the next few years until 1916. (2)

The first changes in the roster came with the purchase of

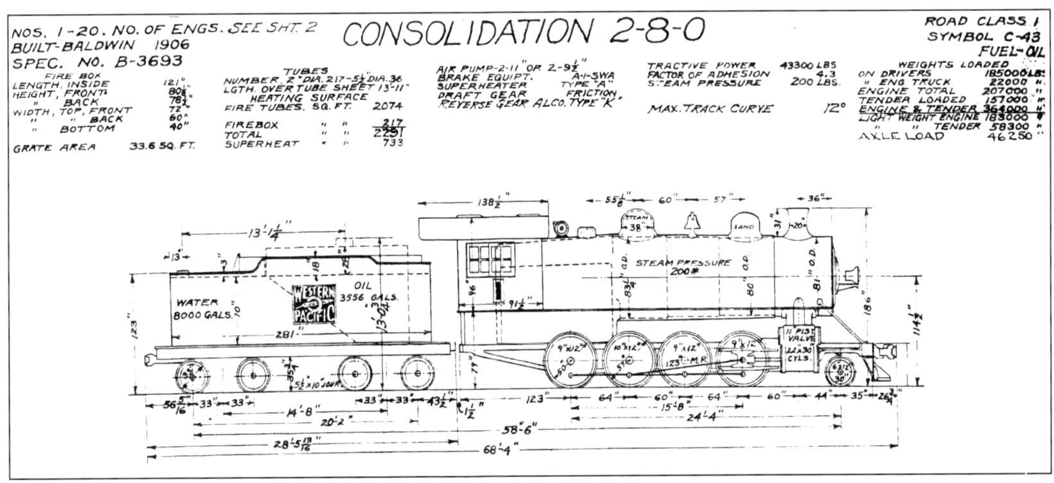

(facing page) Mikado 310 heads up an extra freight in June 1948, demonstrating the modernity of Western Pacific steam power. WP, with its relatively late start in the history of North American railroading, functioned mostly with what might be called "modern steam."

(J. R. Quinn)

(right) Engine 19 illustrates the right-hand side of WP's first class of steam power in November 1947 at Stockton. Note the switcher-style pilot and the tender designed for oil instead of coal.

(Harold K. Vollrath Collection)

(below) Locomotives numbered 1 are usually quite rare, but this 2-8-0 was the first engine of the WP's mainline fleet. Series 1-20 was built by Baldwin in 1906. Seen on the Eastern Division at Delle, Utah, in August 1938. Note the coal in the tender, unlike engine 19.

(Harold K. Vollrath Collection)

the Boca & Loyalton Railroad (the Loyalton Branch). In 1916, the B&L owned seven locomotives, three of which (No. 4, 5, and 7) became WP 123, 124, and 125. The other locomotives were sold and/or scrapped, and in one case, one of the boilers was used as a source of power for construction projects. Two of these engines were 2-8-0 Consolidation types built by Baldwin in 1882, while the third (WP 123) was a Mogul.

In 1917, the WP purchased five more new locomotives from Alco, and two other engines from the Denver and Rio Grande. The used engines were light 4-6-0s numbered 126 and 127. The 126 became Tidewater Southern's number 1 in 1918, and engine 127 became the Deep Creek Railroad's number 2 in 1917.

The five new locomotives purchased in 1917 were the largest powered owned by the WP up to that time. These locomotives were Mallet compounds, 2-6-6-2 type, numbered 201 to 205. (A compound Mallet had one pair of high pressure cylinders and one pair of low pressure cylinders. The low pressure section received steam only after the high pressure cylinders turned the wheels two or three times.) The WP's mechanical department regarded these locomotives as easy steamers.

1918 brought the first five Mikados (2-8-2), which were numbered 301 to 305. This was the first order of such power from Alco, and it would be duplicated in 1919, 1921, 1923, 1924, 1926, and 1929. Up to this time, by the way, nearly all of the steam power was oil burning. However, the first Mikados were coal burners, and so were the 311 to 315 constructed in 1921.

Meanwhile in 1924, the company purchased five more Mallet compounds, numbered 206 to 210. 1927 added four more 0-6-0 switch engines, purchased second-hand from the United Verdi Copper Company in Arizona.

Moving into the depression, the Western Pacific continued to purchase motive power. In 1931 and 1938, the railroad purchased ten 2-8-8-2 Mallets from Baldwin. These were simple (as opposed to compound) in that all four cylinders received steam at boiler pressure. When first delivered, these engines carried 235 pounds of pressure, but this was later boosted to 260 pounds per square inch.

As passenger business was beginning to climb in the mid-1930s, the WP found the aging Ten-wheelers purchased in 1908 and 1909 not quite suitable for the heavier trains. The company could not afford new passenger power, but found what it was looking for on the Florida East Coast Railroad. FEC had ten Mountain type (4-8-2) locomotives for sale: the 403, 404, 405, 406, 407, 408, 410, 412, 414, and 415. These locomotives were purchased by WP in June 1936 and renumbered 171 to 180.

WP purchased seven coal-burning Challenger (4-6-6-4) simple Mallets from Alco in 1938, numbered 401 to 407. The last new steam power came in the midst of the war with six Northerns (4-8-4s) numbered 481 to 486. They were actually part of a Southern Pacific order for semi-streamlined combination freight and passenger power. WP was hard-pressed for locomotives during the war and it is safe to say that if diesels would have been available, these six steamers would not have been purchased. (2)

For the most part, WP did not experiment with their steam power, although they did make minor changes here and there. They tried smoke lifters on the ex-FEC Mountains, but the results were not exactly successful. The Mallets operating on the Western Division were equipped with home-made respirators because there were 33 tunnels on the main line between Oroville and Portola. The longest of these was nearly a mile and a half, and the respirators filtered out smoke and cooled the air. (3)

Steam Operations

One of the limiting factors inherent in mountain operations, even when the maximum grade is only 1 per cent, is the need for helper service. And so it was for the Western Pacific, which could probably be called one of the most carefully planned and built railroads in the United States. There were two principal helper districts on the main line. One was located in the 116-mile Feather River Canyon on the Western Division and the other was the 60-mile Wendover Hill on the Eastern Division.

The ten large 2-8-8-2 Mallets, which had a tractive force with boosters of 150,000 pounds, were assigned to the Western Division. Wendover Hill was assigned the seven Challengers, which had a tractive effort of 96,000 pounds without booster. In peacetime and during the depression, the Mallets were able to handle more of the time freights without helper engines. However, with World War II, helper engine service was imperative. It is interesting to note that in 1942, helper miles represented 17 per cent of the WP's total locomotive miles. (4)

In 1939, prior to the war, WP passenger engines averaged about 150 miles per day, and freight engines just over 100 miles per day. This matched very closely the freight and passenger locomotive crew districts of that time, which had been in effect since 1909. This meant that each locomotive was making only one trip per day. By 1942, the passenger locomotive miles per day had risen to a whopping 254 and freight edged up to 131. (5)

After World War II, WP invested heavily in diesel power and steam was phased out. On March 17, 1950, the final run of steam on the Eastern Division was handled by Ten-wheeler 35. She powered an extra west of empty refrigerator cars. The last steam switcher on the Eastern Division was 164. Her last work was not powering or switching trains, but in standby service for the U.S. Gypsum Company plant at Gerlach, Nevada. By mid-1955, WP was for all practical purposes fully dieselized. Engine 63, a 2-8-0 from the 1909 order, outlasted 44 other locomotives of the same type. In standby service at Stockton, she occasionally handled a local freight. After running 1,026,875 miles, the WP sold her for scrap. (6)

The last steam passenger run was made in 1950 on trains 1 and 2, before the Budd RDCs arrived. The railroad did retain Ten-wheeler 94 for various types of specials. She was repainted in her original scheme in 1954, complete with striping, and was called upon for various activities and celebrations such as powering a special trip of the *California Zephyr* in 1960.

Summary of Western Pacific Steam Power

Symbol	Road Class	Wheel Type	Number Series	Builder	Year
C-43	1	2-8-0	1-20	Baldwin	1906
C-43	21	2-8-0	21-65	Alco	1909
TP-29	71	4-6-0	71-85	Alco	1908
TP-29	86	4-6-0	86-106	Alco	1909
TF-17	121	4-6-0	121, 122	Richmond	1896
C-23	124	2-8-0	124	Baldwin	1882
S-31	151	0-6-0	151-162	Alco	1909
S-34	163	0-6-0	163-166	Alco	1915, 1919
MTP-44	171	4-8-2	171-180	Alco	1924
M-80	201	2-6-6-2	201-205	Alco	1917
M-80	206	2-6-6-2	206-210	Alco	1924
M-137-151	251	2-8-8-2	251-256	Baldwin	1931
M-137-151	257	2-8-8-2	257-260	Baldwin	1938
MK-60	301	2-8-2	301-305	Alco	1918
MK-60	306 *	2-8-2	306-310	Alco	1919
MK-60	311	2-8-2	311-315	Alco	1921
	(1)	2-8-2	321-325		1919
MK-60	316 (2)	2-8-2	316-321	Alco	1923
MK-60-71	322 (2)	2-8-2	322-326	Alco	1924
MK-60-71	327	2-8-2	327-331	Alco	1926
MK-60-71	332	2-8-2	332-336	Alco	1929
M-100	401	4-6-6-4	401-407	Alco	1938
GS-64-77	481	4-8-4	481-486	Lima	1943

*Purchased from USRA in 1920, formerly Elgin, Joliet and Eastern 802-806.

(1) First 321-325 built as USRA light 2-8-2 coal burners; assigned to WP, 1919. Sold to Wabash in1920.
(2) Second group numbered 321-325 purchased in 1923 and 1924, after sale of first group to Wabash.

Source: *Steam Locomotive Equipment Diagrams, Western Pacific Railroad Company.*

Chapter I Endnotes

1 Western Pacific Railroad Mechanical Records
2 Western Pacific Railroad Mechanical Records
3 Western Pacific Railroad Mechanical Records
4 *Railway Age*, 1943, p. 610.
5 *Railway Age*, 1943, p. 610.
6 *Railway Age*, May 9, 1955, p. 8.

TONNAGE RATING

Engine Class	1st Sub-div.	2nd Sub-div.	3rd Sub-div.		4th Sub-div.	Reno Branch	Loyal-ton Branch	Tooele Branch
Eastward								
TP-29....	1170	1950	975		1100	650	1950	420
MTP-44...	2200	4000	1750		2000	....	....	650
C-43......	1800	3600	1500		1700	1100	3000	650
MK-60....	2600	5000	2250		2600	....	....	975
MK-60-71.	2850	5000	2250		2600	....	....	1050
GS-64-77..	2950	5000	2450		2800	....	....	1200
M-100....	....	....	3500		4000	....	....	1500
*D-225.....	4750	6000	4500		5000	....	....	3000
			Wendover to Shafter	**Shafter to Hogan**				
Westward								
TP-29....	1040	1950	780	930	1100	420	1950	1950
MTP-44...	1850	4000	1350	1620	1850	....	....	3000
C-43......	1600	3600	1150	1380	1600	650	3000	3000
MK-60....	2200	5000	1750	2100	2400	....	....	5000
MK-60-71.	2450	5000	1800	2200	2500	....	....	5000
GS-64-77..	2550	5000	1950	2400	2600	....	....	5000
M-100....	....	....	2850	3300	3800	....	....	8000
*D-225.....	4500	6500	4250	4500	4750	....	....	10000

***Reduce 25% of tonnage rating for each inoperative Diesel unit.**

To determine tonnage for helper trains, 1st, 3rd and 4th Subdivisions and Branches, add together tonnage rating for class of engines furnished.

Add five tons friction for each car over 30 cars.

Tonnage rating based on maximum grade each Subdivision; between points where grades are less than maximum, greater tonnage can be handled.

(right) Information on steam tonnage ratings from WP's Eastern Division Timetable No. 41, July 6, 1947, p.16. Class D-255 are FT diesel road locomotives.

To 2-8-0 35 (series 21-65) goes the distinction of being the last steamer to operate on the Eastern Division. This photo, taken at Portola in 1938, illustrates such unusual features as the brakeman's doghouse on the tender and the huge plow – added for winter operation. See diagram road class 21, symbol C-43.

(Bob Larson Collection)

NOS. 21-65. NO. OF ENGS. SEE SHT. 1-B
BUILT-ALCO. 1909
SPEC. NO. A-3920-B

CONSOLIDATION 2-8-0

ROAD CLASS 21
SYMBOL C-43
FUEL - OIL

FIREBOX
LENGTH, INSIDE 121"
HEIGHT, FRONT 80½"
" BACK 78⅝"
WIDTH, TOP, FRONT 72"
" " BACK 60"
" BOTTOM 40"

TUBES
NUMBER, 2" DIA. 217 - 5½" DIA. 36
LGTH. OVER TUBE SHEET 13'-11"
HEATING SURFACE
FIRE TUBES, SQ. FT. 2074
FIREBOX " " 218
TOTAL " " 2292
SUPERHEAT " " 733

AIR PUMP-2-11" OR 1-8½" C.C.
BRAKE EQUIPT. ET-6, & WN-2
SUPERHEATER TYPE "A"
DRAFT GEAR FRICTION
REVERSE GEAR ALCO. TYPE "K"

TRACTIVE POWER 43300 LBS
FACTOR OF ADHESION 4.24
STEAM PRESSURE 200 LBS.
MAX. TRACK CURVE 12°

WEIGHTS LOADED
ON DRIVERS 184000 LBS
" ENG. TRUCK 19000 "
ENGINE, TOTAL 203000 "
TENDER, LOADED 155000 "
ENGINE & TENDER 358000 "
LIGHT WEIGHT, ENGINE 179000 "
" " TENDER 60300 "
AXLE LOAD 46000 "

NOTE -
ENGINES NOS. 39, 44 & 59
ARE NOT EQUIPPED WITH SUPERHEATER.

WATER 8000 GALS.
OIL 3000 GALS.
STEAM PRESSURE 200#
21

For a comprehensive look at both sides of a Western Pacific 2-8-0, we have number 60. The left side was snapped in 1939, while the right-hand view was taken in 1946.

(Both, Harold K. Vollrath Collection)

The next group of WP power came in the form of Ten-wheelers, series 71 to 85.

(Bob Larson Collection)

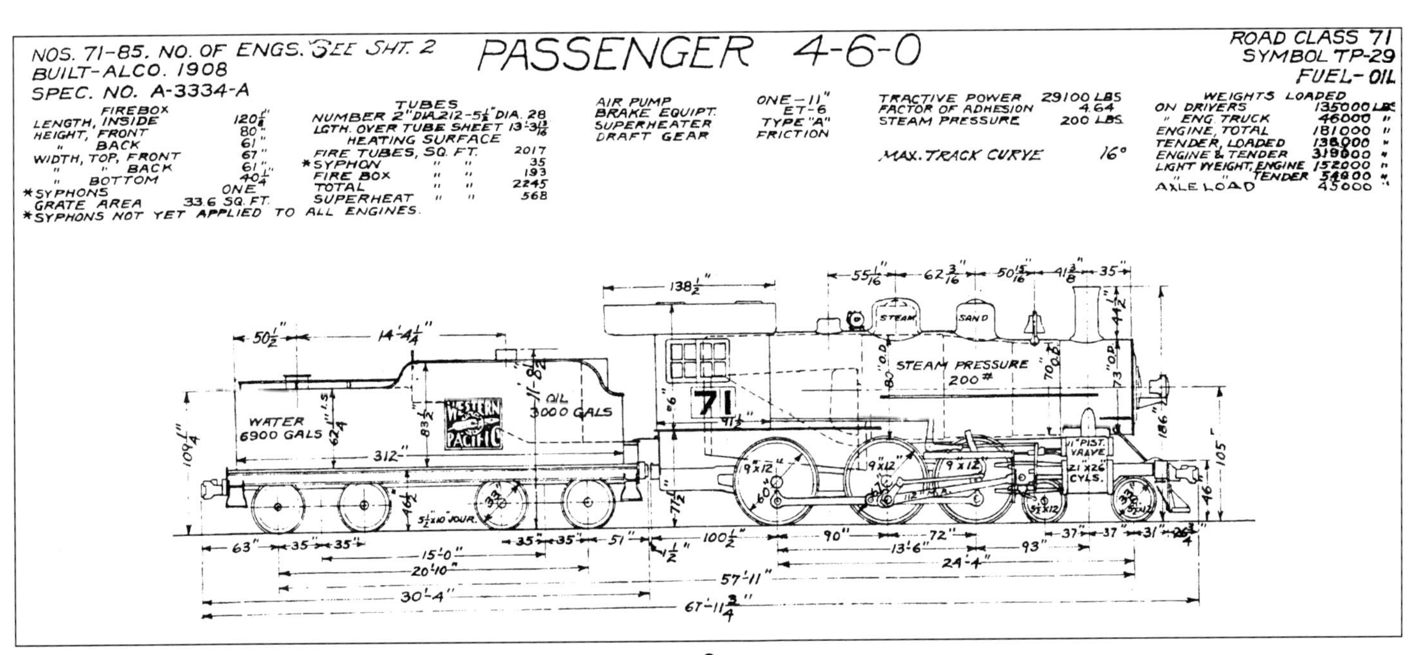

(above) It appears that 77 is in dead storage in this 1949 view at Oakland, California. This photo illustrates the left side of these compact locomotives.

(Harold K. Vollrath Collection)

(below) The second group of Ten-wheelers (series 86-106) were built in 1909. Note the differences between 89 and engine 77 shown above. 89 was photographed in storage at Stockton in September 1948.

(Harold K. Vollrath Collection)

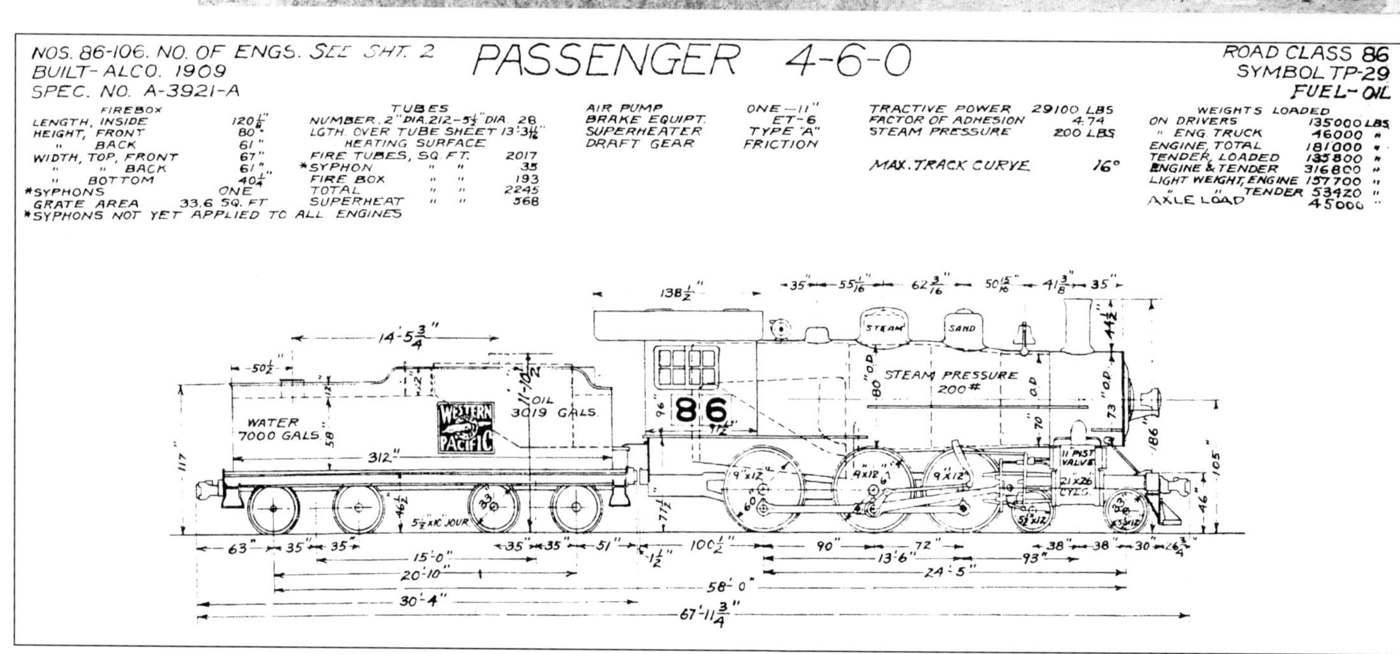

94 became the most famous of all WP Ten-wheelers after being repainted in the original lettering scheme and used for various celebrations and promotions. Seen here in her restored original dress in October 1954 – 45 years after construction!

(Harold K. Vollrath Collection)

How did the 94 look before her reincarnation? This 1948 view at Stockton shows a very modern and business-like 4-6-0. Note the bolted-on cab number and tender insignia, typical features of WP steam power.

(Bob Lorenz Collection)

106 was the last of the WP Ten-wheelers. After having been bumped from mainline passenger duties by heavier 4-8-2s, they worked local freights until the late 1940s. 106 is shown here in storage at Salt Lake City in October 1947.

(Author's Collection)

Ten-wheeler 99 shows the left side of the Road Class 86 engines at Stockton in August 1947.

(J.R. Quinn)

Built by Richmond in 1896 as Alameda & San Joaquin number 2, WP 122 (along with sister 121) retained the original "short line atmosphere" with its rectangular tender, tall stack, arch-bar trucks and small boiler. Shown at Stockton, California, in October 1948.

(Harold K. Vollrath Collection)

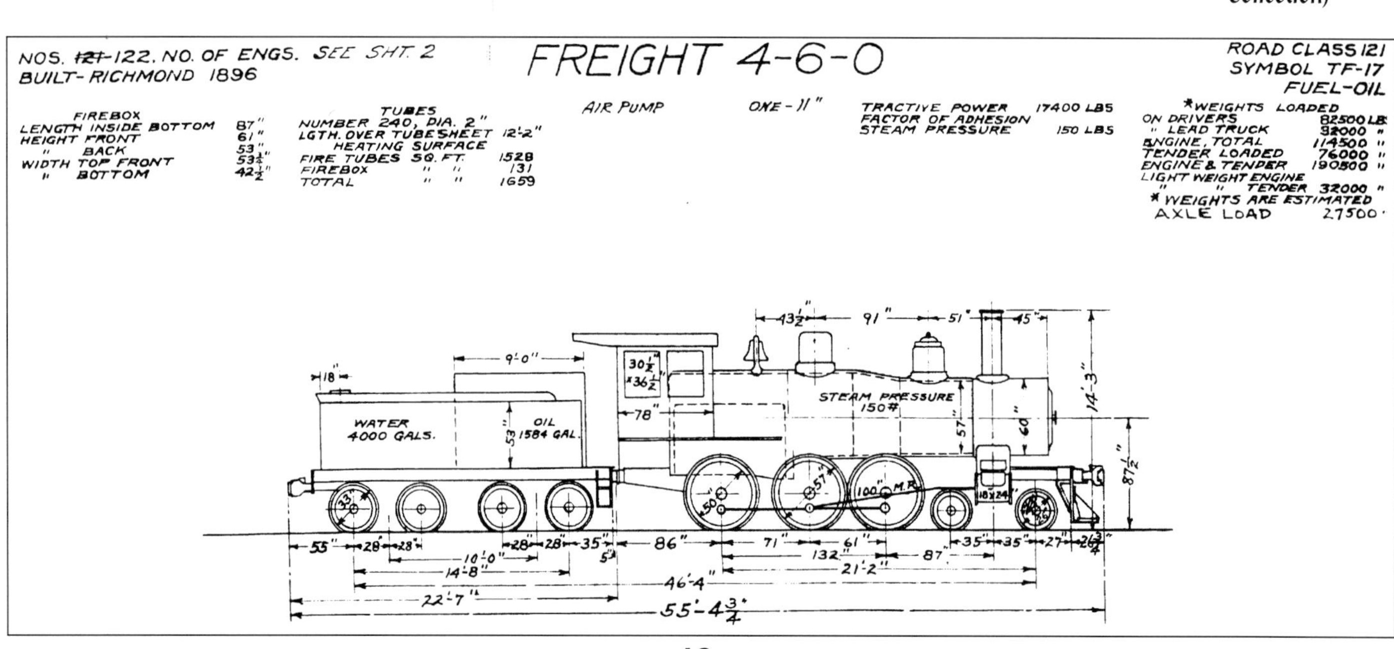

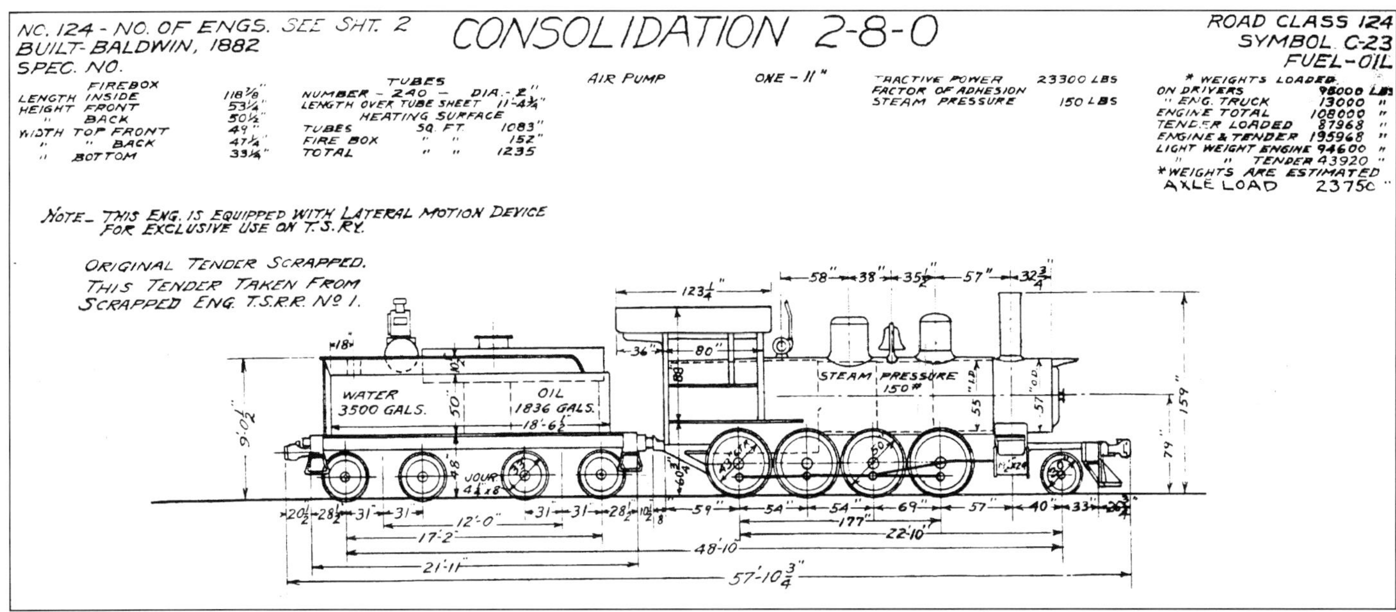

One-of-a-kind on the WP was 124, a 2-8-0 built by Baldwin in 1882 for the Boca & Loyalton. This little engine has something of a narrow gauge look. Photographed at Stockton, June 1941.
(Harold K. Vollrath Collection)

Western Pacific operated a reliable fleet of 0-6-0s, numbered from 151 to 166, built by Alco between 1909 and 1919. They handled classification, pick-up and delivery work for the WP for several decades. In the case of the 151 it is steaming softly, waiting for its crew and next assignment at Stockton in October 1948.
(Harold K. Vollrath Collection)

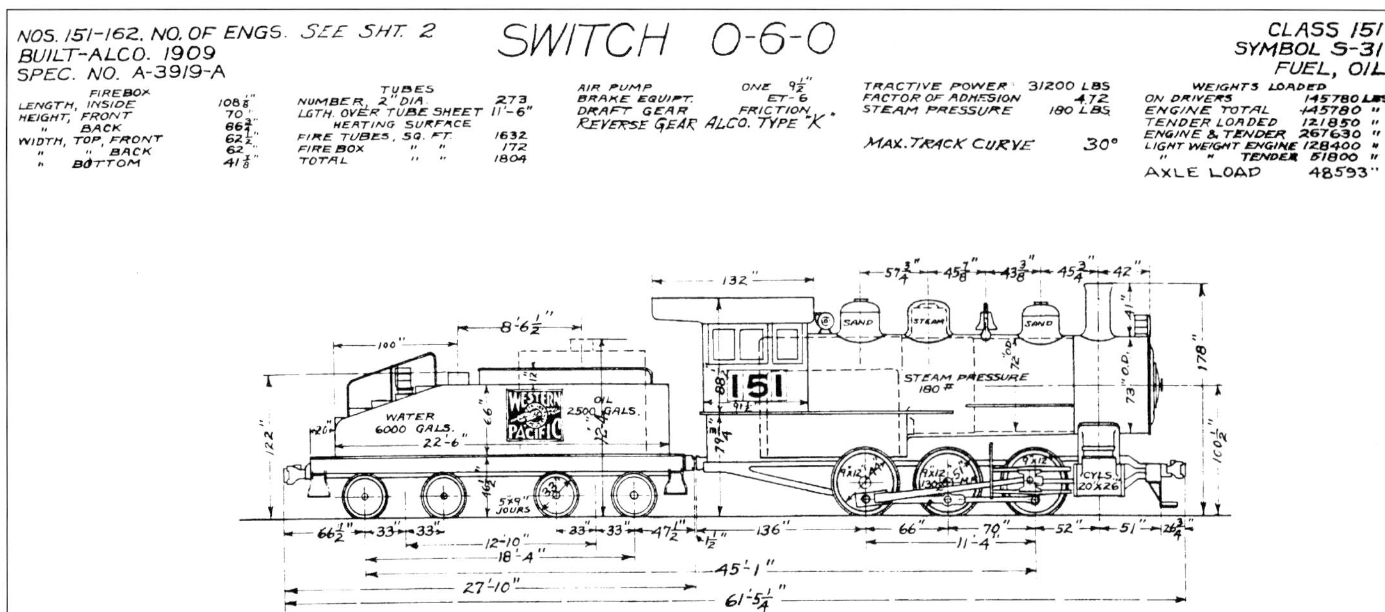

A right side view of the 0-6-0 152 at Stockton, California, on July 31, 1952.
(J. R. Quinn)

Steam tonnage ratings from WP's Western Division Timetable No. 35, July 6, 1947, p. 21.

TONNAGE RATING

Engine Class	1st Sub-division	2nd Sub-division	3rd Sub-division	4th Subdivision		
				Keddie to Greenville	Greenville to Almanor	Almanor to Bieber
Eastward						
TP-29....	1073	2200	812	585	401	585
MTP-44....	1650	5000	1250	900	617	900
C-43....	1650	5000	1250	900	617	900
MK-60....	2500	6000	1800	1250	858	1250
MK-60-71..	2700	6000	1800	1250	858	1250
GS-64-77..	2800	6000	1900	1250	858	1250
M-80....	3000	6000	2200	1690	1170	1690
M-137-151	5000	6000	4000	2800	1900	2800
D-225...	5800	6000	4000	3400	2000	3400
				Bieber to Halls Flat	Halls Flat to Keddie	
Westward						
TP-29....	910	2200	*	491	1040	
MTP-44....	1400	5000	*	756	1600	
C-43....	1400	5000	*	756	1600	
MK-60....	2350	6000	*	1051	2200	
MK-60-71..	2500	6000	*	1051	2350	
GS-64-77..	2500	6000	*	1051	2450	
M-80....	2600	6000	*	1427	3500	
M-137-151	4000	6000	*	2200	5500	
D-225...	5000	6000	*	2800	6000	

***Descending grade, no tonnage limit.**
Add five tons friction for each car over 30 cars.
Tonnage rating based on maximum grade each subdivision; between points where grades are less than maximum, greater tonnage can be handled.

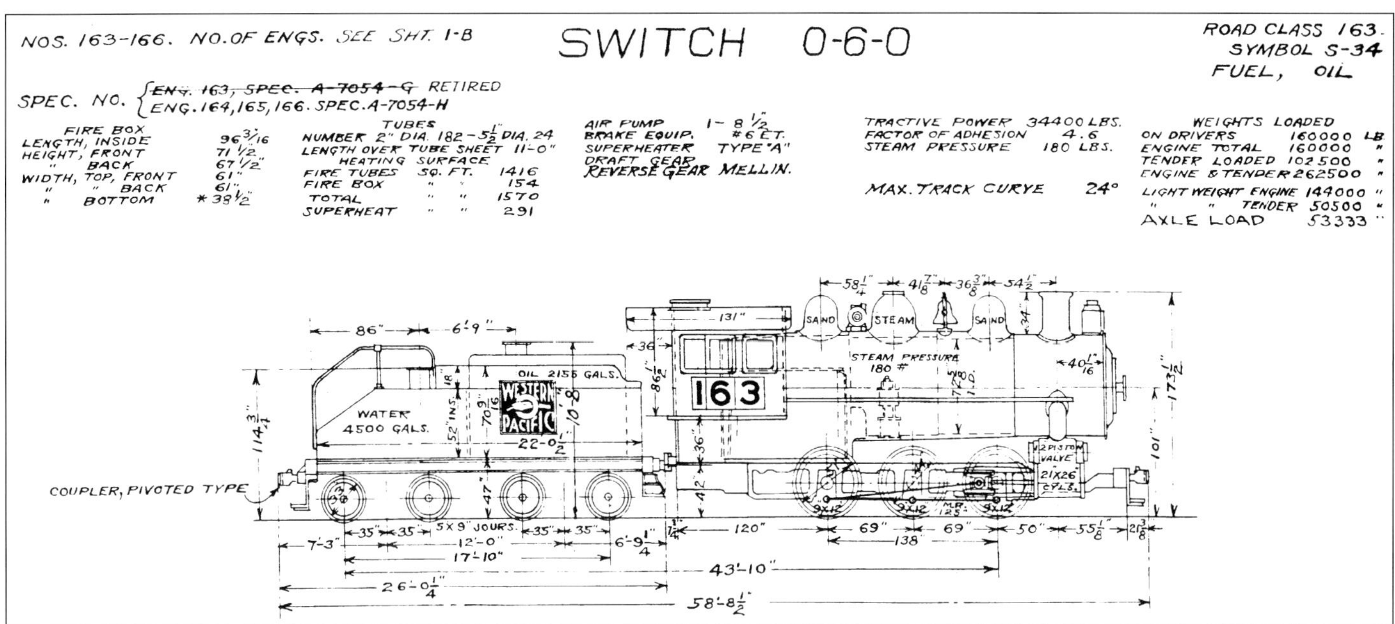

(left) Freshly painted WP 0-6-0 164.

(below) 164 was the last steamer to run between Gerlach and Portola, in August 1954. She is covered with the stains and strains of switching U. S. Gypsum's Gerlach facility. Note the different headlight. Although out of service, 164 was not retired until 1957 and was ultimately placed on display at Oroville.

(Bob Larson Collection)

(above) Mountains 171-180 were purchased from Florida East Coast. 172 is seen at Stockton in November 1948.

(left) 177 (ex-FEC 410) was at Oroville on July 26, 1938.
(Both, Bob Larson Collection)

172 had a smoke deflector in this January 1939 view at Niles, California.
(Harold K. Vollrath Collection)

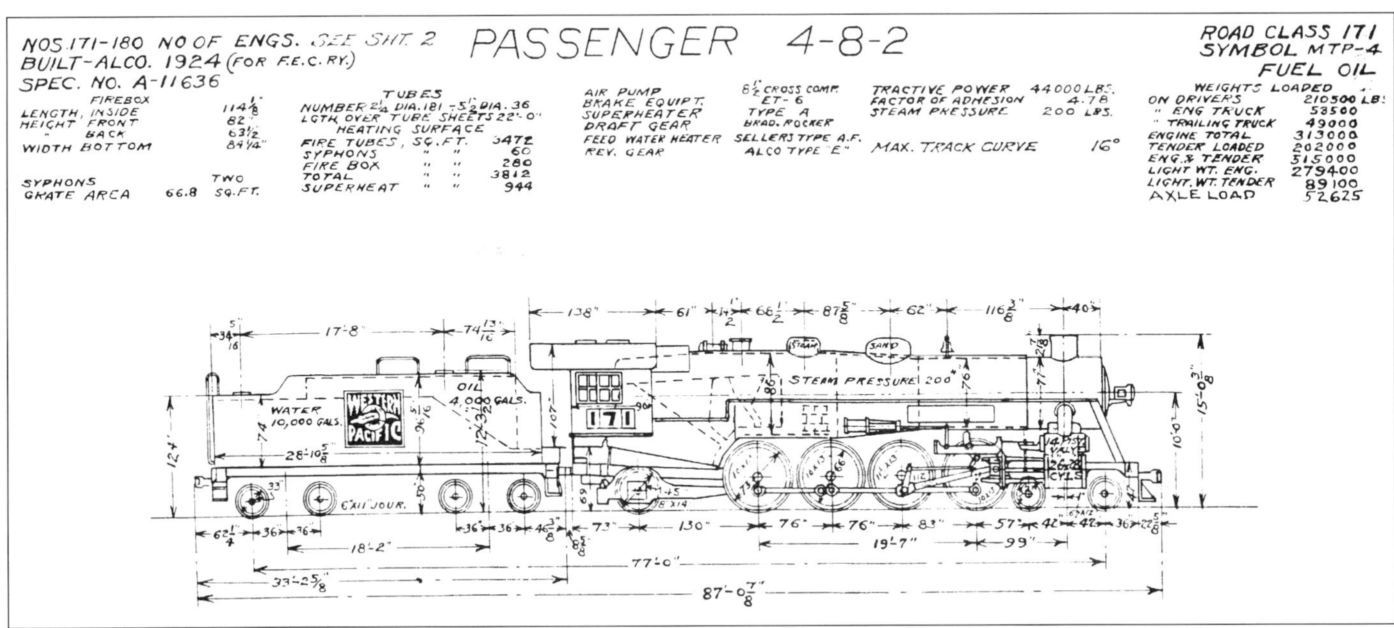

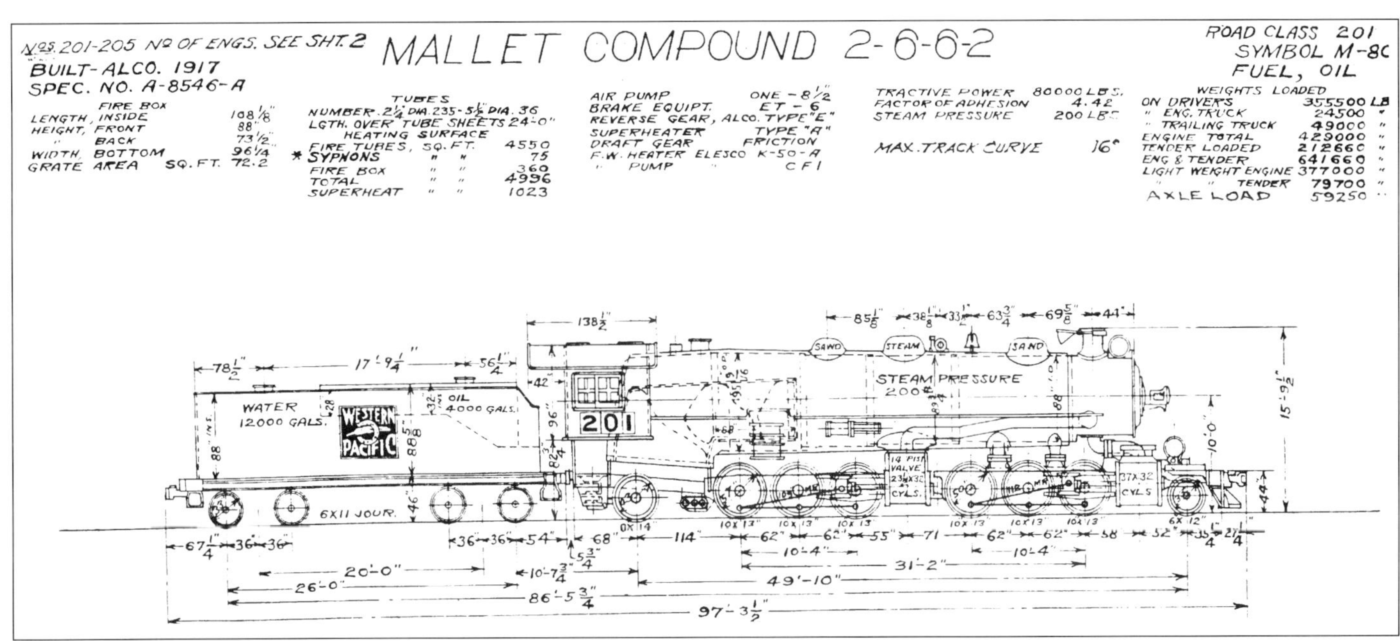

The Western Pacific was a mainline railroad with steep mountain grades. Consequently, Mallets in the form of 2-6-6-2s arrived on the railroad in two groups, 201-205 in 1917, and 206-210 in 1924. This left side view of the 202 was taken at Keddie, California, in July 1939. *(Harold K. Vollrath Collection)*

2-6-6-2 Mallet 202 was photographed at Keddie in July 1949 after it had been taken out of service. Note the cap on the stack.

(Harold K. Vollrath Collection)

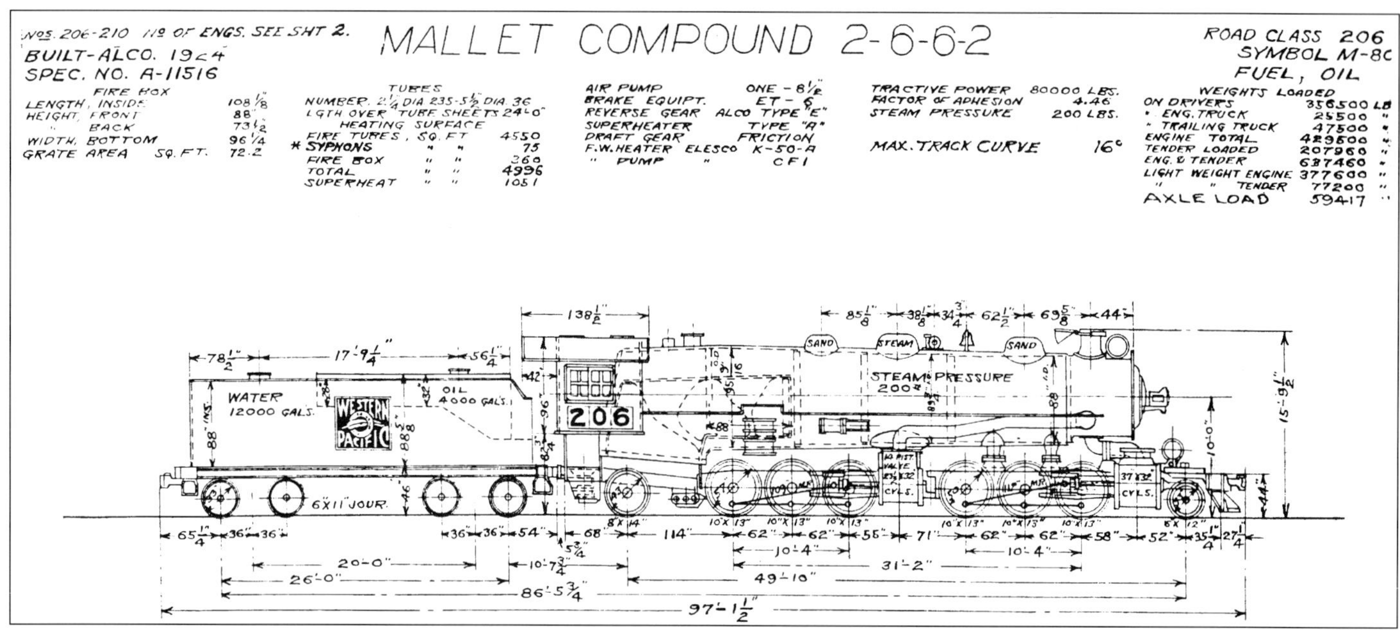

The sun was shining just right on the 209 for the various details to show up. Seen in service at Keddie in July 1946.

(Harold K. Vollrath Collection)

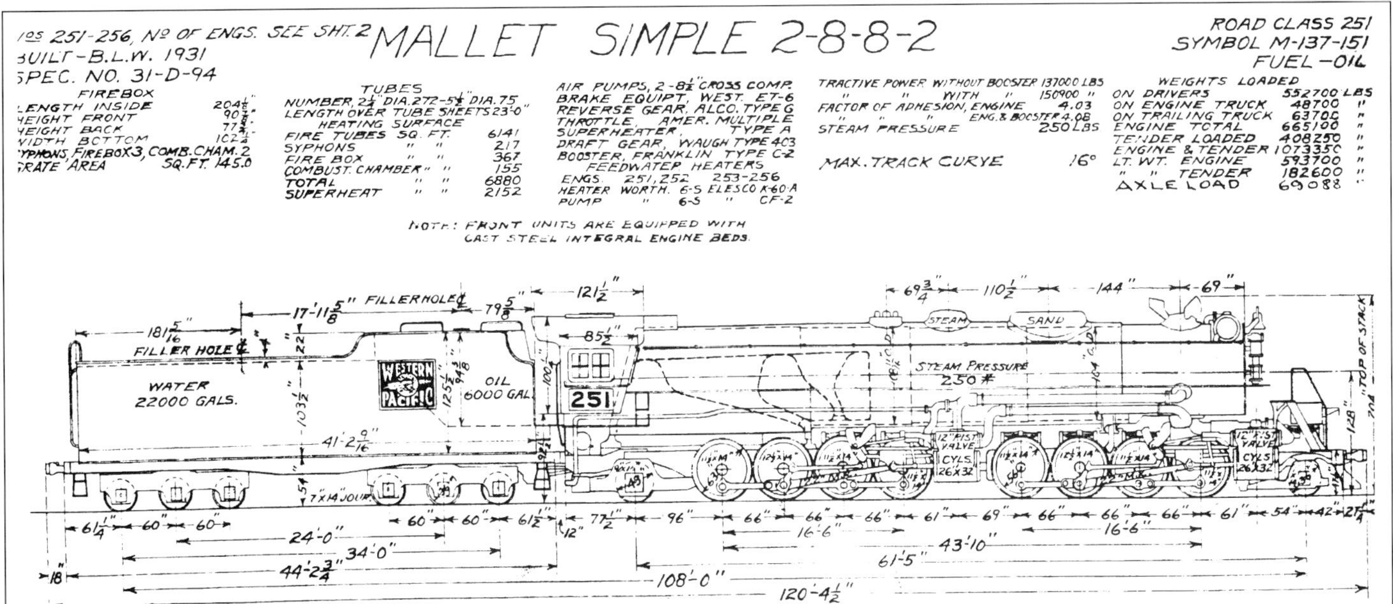

(right) WP's largest Mallets were two groups of 2-8-8-2s, numbered 251-256 (Baldwin, 1931), and 257-260 (Baldwin, 1938). 252 was in service at Keddie in August 1949.

(below) Air pumps on the smokebox added to the massive look of these 2-8-8-2s. The 259 is being sanded at Portola's engine terminal in July 1948.

(Both, Harold K. Vollrath Collection)

MISCELLANEOUS

DOUBLEHEADING.

First Subdivision—Engines heavier than one Mallet (M-100 Class) and one Consolidation (C-43 Class) must not be doubleheaded between Portola and Doyle.

Second Subdivision—Two Mallet engines (SP or WP) or two SP engines heavier than SP Class F-3, 4 and 5, must not be doubleheaded between Weso and Elko, except that two SP "GS" type engines may be doubleheaded between Carlin and Elko.

Third Subdivision—Two Mallet engines (SP or WP) or two WP engines heavier than one Mallet (M-100 Class) and one Consolidation (C-43 Class), or two SP engines heavier than "GS" type must not be doubleheaded between Elko and SP Connection (MP 701).

When two Mallet or two engines heavier than those specified above are handling trains (or being towed) in above territories, they must be separated by five (5) cars.

When a TP-29 engine is doubleheaded on a passenger train over a passenger district with another engine of greater pump capacity it should be placed next to train. When used as a helper over part of the passenger district it should be placed in the lead.

(From WP Eastern Division Timetable No. 41, July 6, 1947, p. 15)

(above) The second batch of 2-8-8-2s was delivered in April 1938. Minus rods, the spanking new 259 gleams in the sunlight at Missouri Pacific's East St. Louis yard during its shipment west.

(Harold K. Vollrath Collection)

(below) Compare this photo of the 257 with that of 252 on the previous page. There were several modifications to the steam pipe arrangement and placement, and other subtle differences between the two groups of motive power. Oroville, August 13, 1949.

(J. R. Quinn)

Despite the fact that WP owned and operated only 36 2-8-2 Mikados, they arrived in six different groups during 1918, 1919, 1921, 1923, 1924, 1926 and 1929. 301 was the first of this group of engines. There were some minor differences among the 36 Mikados. For instance, the 301 (301-305) carried its bell behind the stack. Yet, of course, they all had the same general appearance. Seen at Stockton in September 1951.
(Harold K. Vollrath Collection)

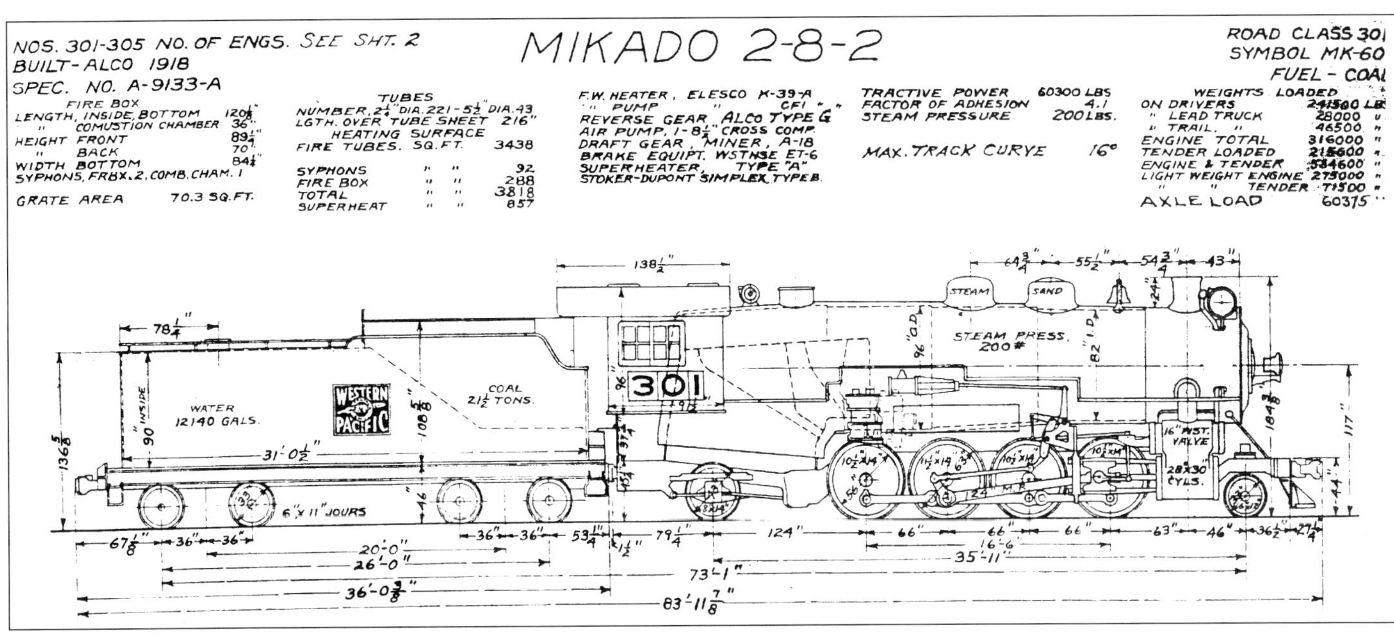

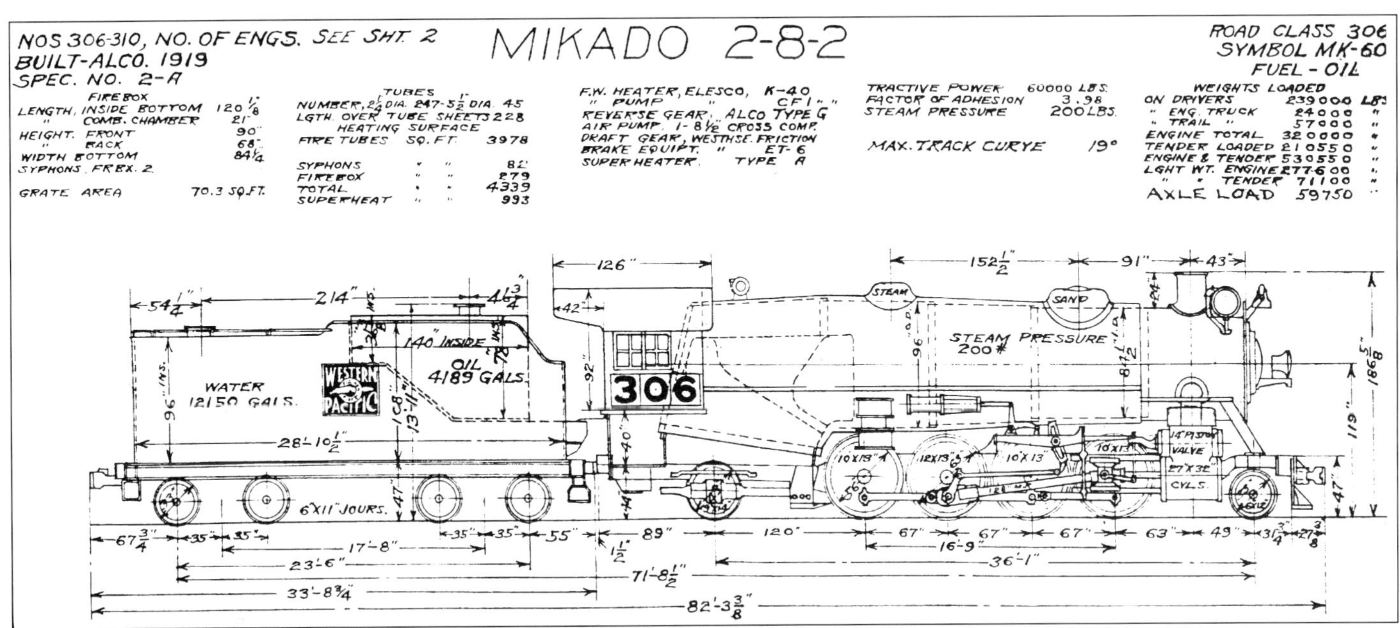

WP 307 (306-310) carried its bell at the top of the smokebox and ahead of the feedwater heater. 307 and her sisters within the group were actually purchased from the USRA, and were former Elgin, Joliet & Eastern coal burning heavy Mikes 802-806. Seen at Stockton, California, July 1948.
(Harold K. Vollrath Collection)

Left-side view of 307 taken at Sacramento in November 1941.
(Harold K. Vollrath Collection)

(below) 312 was part of group 311-315. There are a number of differences, besides the tender, such as the placement of the steam dome and the bell. As coal burners they worked on the Eastern Division for their entire careers. Seen at Salt Lake City in May 1946.
(Harold K. Vollrath Collection)

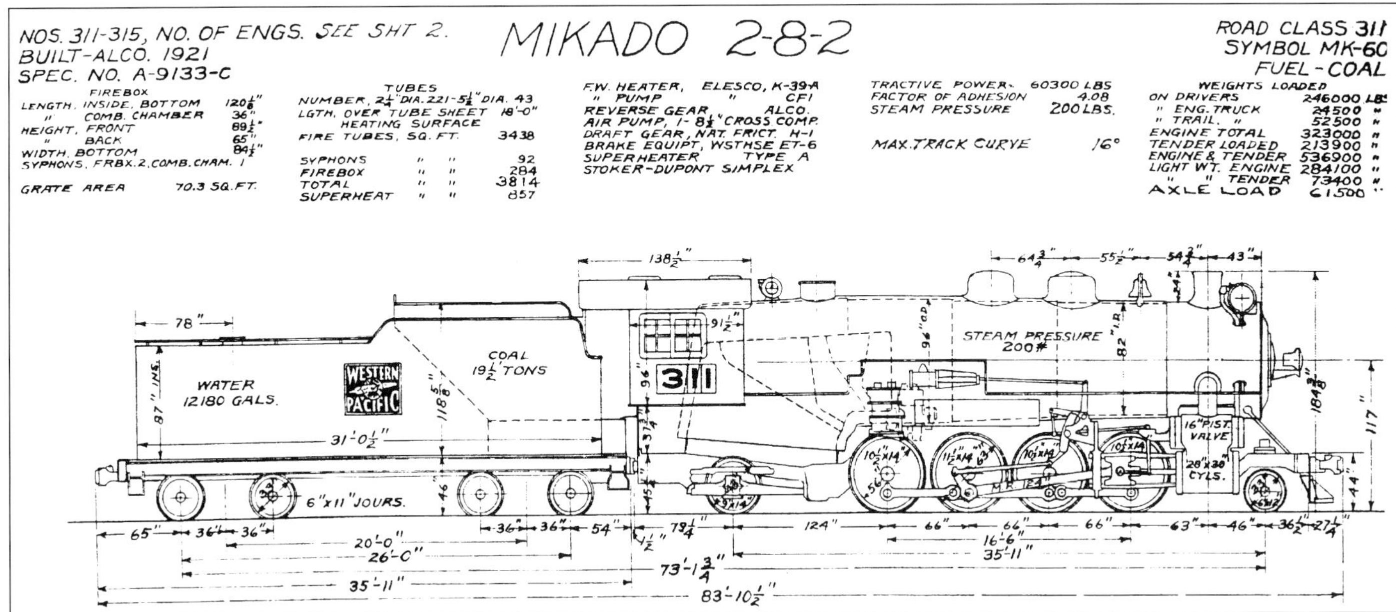

WP 316 (316-321) was built in 1923. Originally this group of power was constructed without the Elesco feedwater heaters. The engines also received head-end brakeman's cabins (doghouses) on their tenders. Seen at Stockton in July 1948. *(Harold K. Vollrath Collection)*

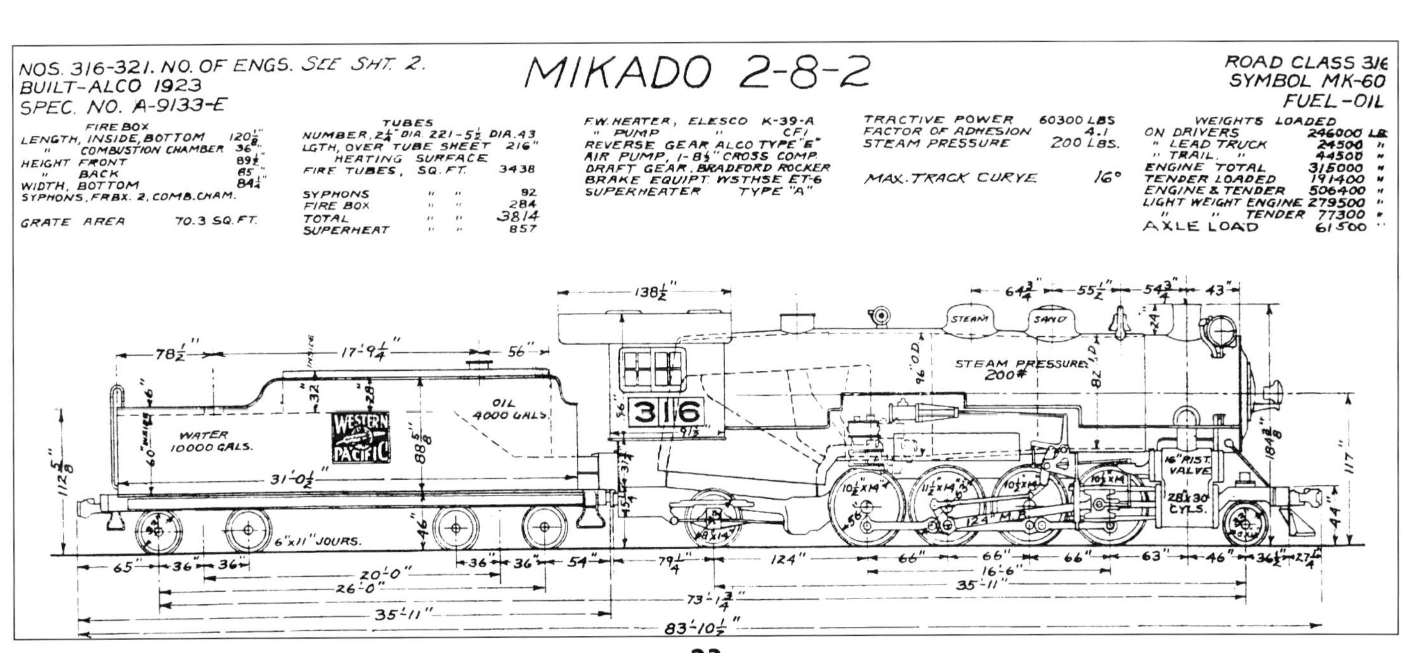

(above) Mikado 320 was the second-last engine in Road Class 316. Stockton, March 1949.

(J. R. Quinn)

(left) 324, at Stockton on July 3, 1940, illustrates the right side of Road Class 322 with an Elesco feedwater heater.

(J. R. Quinn)

(left) 322 was not equipped with a feedwater heater. It was part of group 322-326, all equipped with 10,000 gallon tenders. The engine is being readied for an extra freight at Stockton, California, in November 1947.

(Harold K. Vollrath Collection)

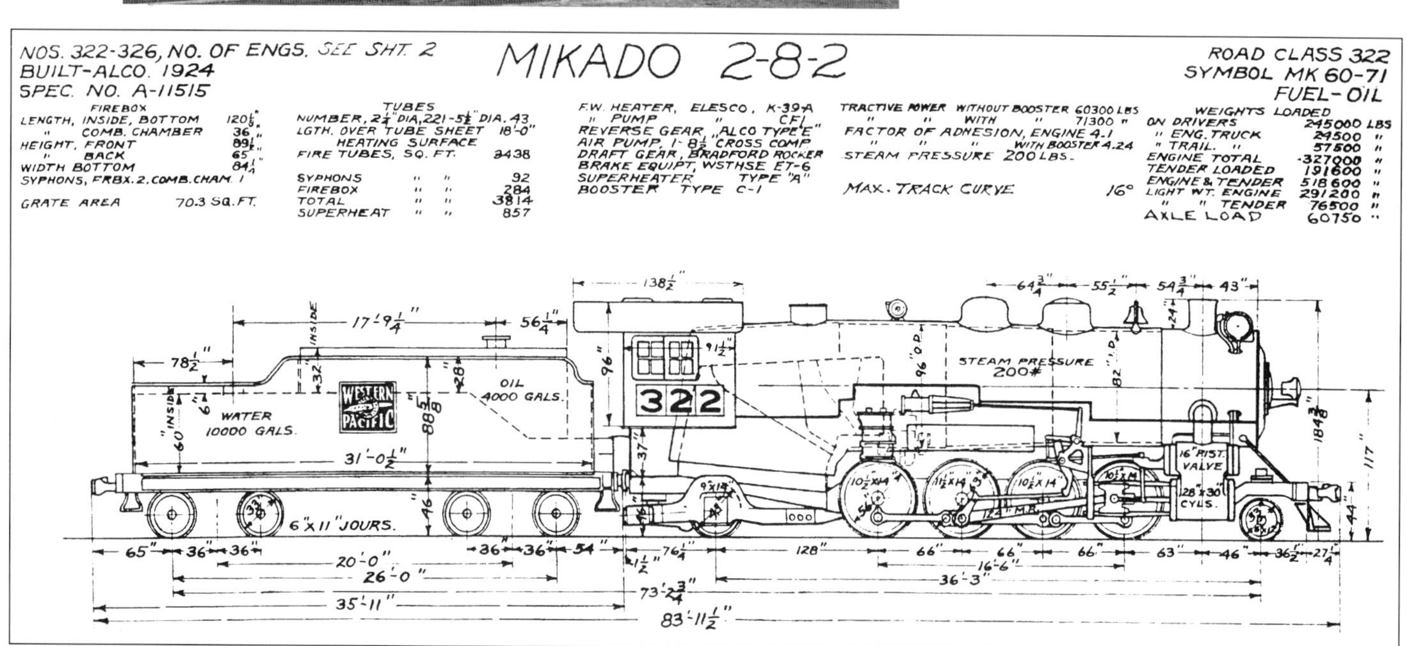

(right) Mikado 331 was part of the second-last group (327-331). Virtually identical to the final group, 332-336, they had 15,000 gallon tenders which gave them an additional massive appearance. 331 has just about seen its days as it waits in storage at Stockton in April 1953.

(below) Right side of 331, in service at Stockton in April 1950.

(Both, Harold K. Vollrath Collection)

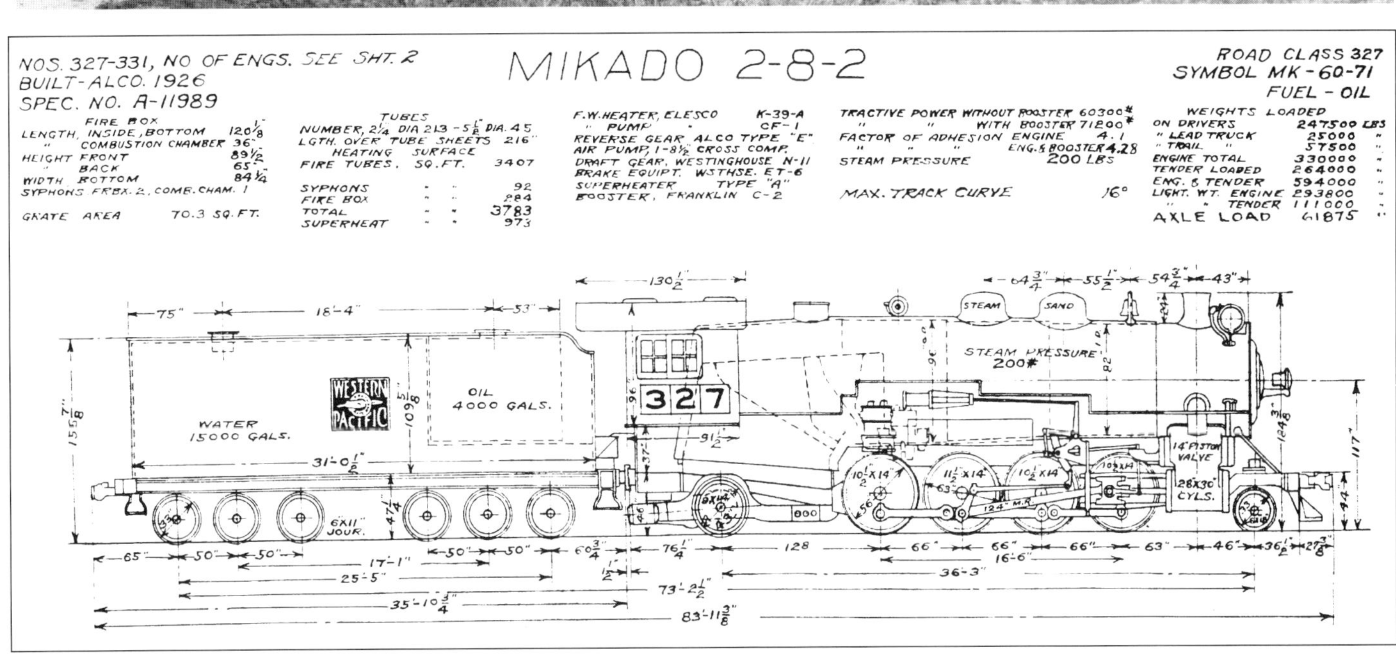

(left) 336 was the very last WP 2-8-2 built, but it was not the last Mikado on the railroad – that distinction goes to 334. 336 is seen at Stockton in January 1954, after official retirement in 1953.
(Harold K. Vollrath Collection)

(below) 334 had the honor of being the last operating 2-8-2 on the WP. Although officially retired in 1955, it was reactivated in early 1956 and handled passenger extras during 1957. 334 was eventually repainted and moved to Rio Vista Junction for display in 1967. Seen at Fremont, California, on a March 18, 1956, passenger extra.
(J. R. Quinn)

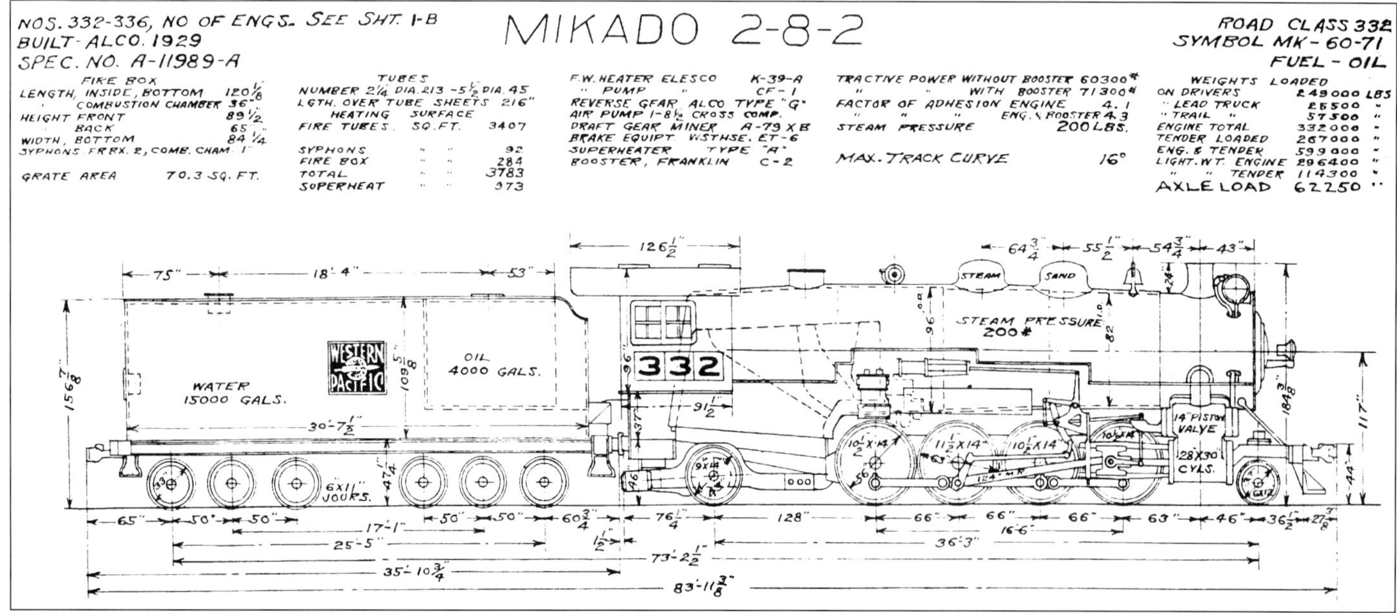

(above) WP purchased coal-fired 4-6-6-4 Challengers 401-407 in 1938 for time freight service between Salt Lake City and Elko. These massive engines saw but 12 years of service on the WP. 401, seen at Elko in August 1949, also operated on the Union Pacific in late 1950. WP offered these engines to several roads, including GN, without success.

(left) 407 being coaled at Wendover, Utah, in May 1949.
(Both, Harold K. Vollrath Collection)

(below) 402 at Oakland on April 1, 1946. *(J.R. Quinn)*

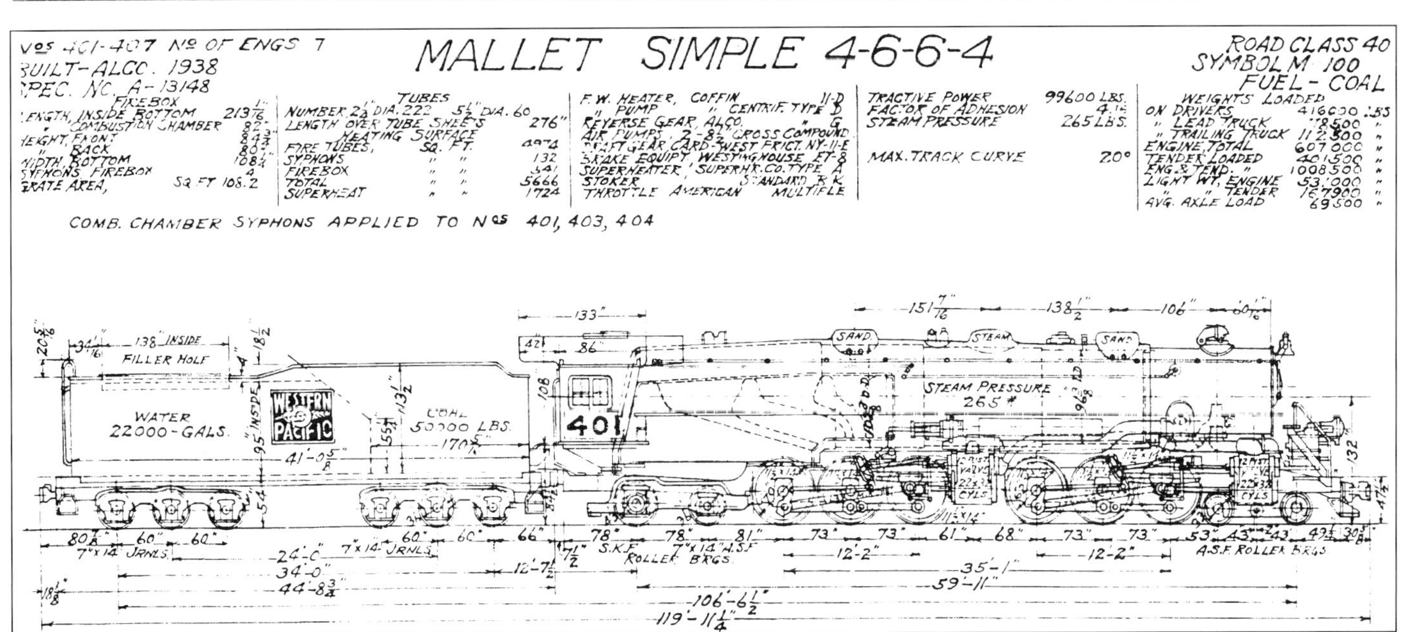

481

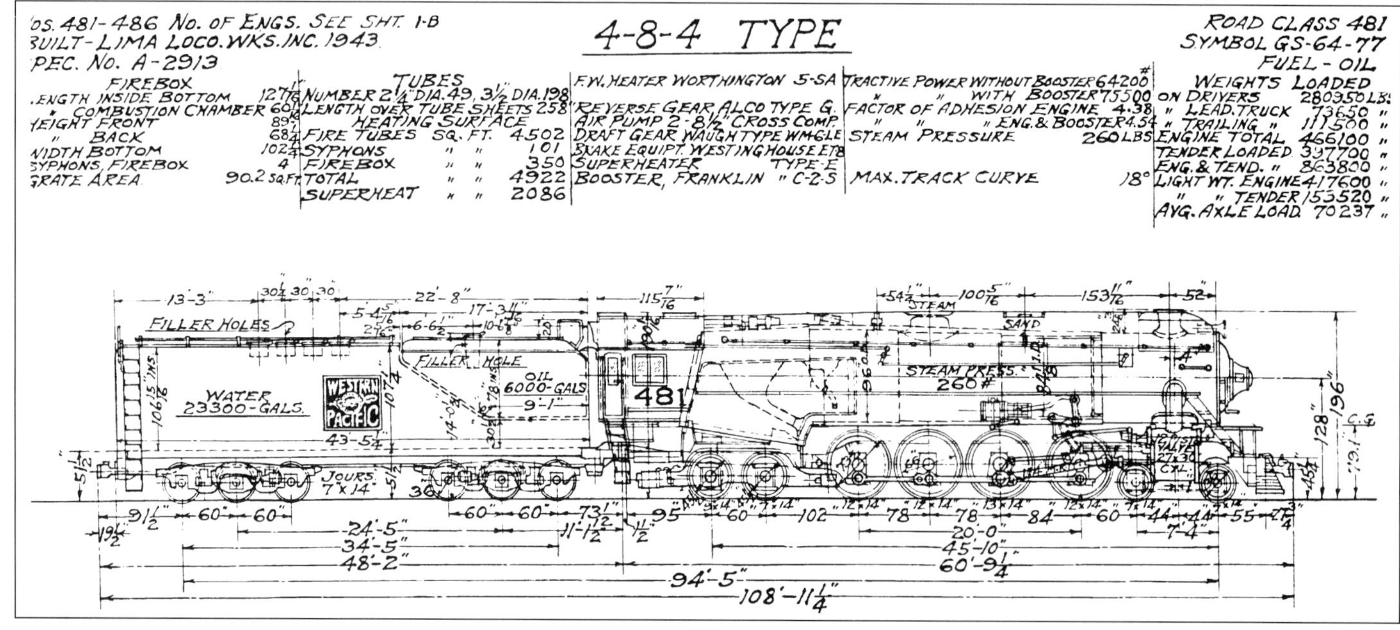
'OS. 481-486 No. OF ENGS. SEE SHT. 1-B
BUILT-LIMA LOCO. WKS. INC. 1943
PEC. No. A-2913
4-8-4 TYPE
ROAD CLASS 481
SYMBOL GS-64-77
FUEL - OIL
FIREBOX
LENGTH INSIDE BOTTOM 127 7/16
" COMBUSTION CHAMBER 60 1/16
HEIGHT FRONT 89 1/2
" BACK 68 1/4
WIDTH BOTTOM 102 1/4
SYPHONS, FIREBOX 4
GRATE AREA 90.2 SQ. FT.
TUBES
NUMBER 2 1/4" DIA. 49, 3 1/2" DIA. 198
LENGTH OVER TUBE SHEETS 258"
HEATING SURFACE
FIRE TUBES SQ. FT. 4502
SYPHONS " " 101
FIREBOX " " 350
TOTAL " " 4922
SUPERHEAT " " 2086
F.W. HEATER WORTHINGTON 5-SA
REVERSE GEAR ALCO TYPE G.
AIR PUMP 2-8 1/2" CROSS COMP.
DRAFT GEAR WAUGH TYPE WM-6-LE
BRAKE EQUIPT. WESTINGHOUSE ET8
SUPERHEATER TYPE-E
BOOSTER, FRANKLIN " C-2-S
TRACTIVE POWER WITHOUT BOOSTER 64200#
" " WITH BOOSTER 75500
FACTOR OF ADHESION ENGINE 4.38
" " " ENG. & BOOSTER 4.54
STEAM PRESSURE 260 LBS
MAX. TRACK CURVE 18°
WEIGHTS LOADED
ON DRIVERS 280950 LBS
" LEAD. TRUCK 73650 "
" TRAILING " 111500 "
ENGINE TOTAL 466100 "
TENDER LOADED 397700 "
ENG. & TEND. " 863800 "
LIGHT WT. ENGINE 417600 "
" " TENDER 155520 "
AVG. AXLE LOAD 70237 "
FILLER HOLES
WATER 23300-GALS.
FILLER HOLE
OIL 6000-GALS
STEAM
SAND
STEAM PRESS. 260#
481
WESTERN PACIFIC
JOURS. 7 X 14
94'-5"
108'-11 1/4"

(facing page, top) WP's last steam locomotives were six semi-streamlined 4-8-4 Northerns, built by Lima in 1943 as part of a Southern Pacific order. These "almost Daylights" worked passenger and freight trains for about ten years. Smoke deflectors were fitted after World War II, as seen on 482 handling a passenger extra at Oroville in September 1948.
(Harold K. Vollrath Collection)

(facing page, middle) 481 shows its SP design heritage.
(J. R. Quinn)

(above) Seven-year-old Northern 482 photographed in service at Stockton in August 1950.
(Harold K. Vollrath Collection)

(below) 485 shows off her brand-new appearance in passenger service at Salt Lake City on October 4, 1944.
(Bob Larson Collection)

2 Diesel Locomotives

FTs 901A and 908D and F7s 923A and 916A (left to right) are on the lineup at Stockton, California, the day after Christmas in 1958. *(Bob Larson Collection)*

The Western Pacific purchased its first diesel locomotive, an Electro-Motive SW1 switch engine, in 1939. The company's first road power, in the form of Electro-Motive FTs, arrived in 1941 – just about two years before delivery of the company's last modern steam power. The first diesel passenger power for the heavyweight *Exposition Flyer* arrived in 1947, with additional passenger locomotives arriving in 1948 and 1950 for service on the *Flyer's* replacement, the *California Zephyr*. Meanwhile, the company continued to purchase not only the reliable FT, but also F3s and F7s as they were developed.

Western Pacific was highly impressed with its first FTs during those early war years. They used them as a "flying squadron" on any part of the railroad where they were needed. In 1942, the road diesels were placed under a progressive maintenance system. The FTs were able to make a round trip between Oroville and Salt Lake City, a distance of 1,450 miles, without any problem at all. As soon as they arrived at Oroville, they would be sent east again to Portola, and back again, a distance of 232 miles. On their return trip to Oroville, they would be placed in the shop for any necessary maintenance work. At the time it was believed that the periodical maintenance would avoid frequent general overhauling and thus greater utilization could be obtained from the locomotives (1). This turned out to be true during those early days of dieselization on the WP.

From 1939 through 1953, the WP purchased a fleet of switch engines, road switchers and road engines (the various F models mentioned earlier) that replaced all but a handful of the steam power. A few steam

(above) The smallest switchers on the Western Pacific were the 600 h.p. SW1s from EMC (1939), series 501-503. This photo illustrates the silver and orange scheme with the striping placement on the front end.
(Bob Larson Collection)

(right) In 1959, the Oakland Yard had five switch engines on the 3:59 p.m. shift. Starting with the 557, they were all lined up and ready to go on a January afternoon.
(Bob Larson Collection)

(below) There were eight 660 h.p. Alco S1s in series 504-511. The silver and orange scheme fit these units quite well, with its prominent Western Pacific lettering.
(Bob Larson Collection)

(above) Western Pacific's 660 h.p. S1 switchers were built in 1942, and were originally painted black with white striping and lettering. Indeed, note the words "Feather River Route" on the side of the unit below the road name. Of the early switchers, the EMC SW1s never carried the safety stripes, as illustrated on S1 509.
(Bob Larson Collection)

(left) It is May 31, 1969, and WP's Alco S1 505 has been leased to the Stockton Terminal and Eastern at Stockton. The unit is in the solid orange color scheme.
(Collection of the Author)

engines lasted until 1956 when their flue dates ran out, and then the diesel was undisputed king on WP.

Western Pacific road power was originally painted in a very attractive yellow and green color scheme. This was eventually replaced with the equally attractive orange and silver scheme. The road experimented with a solid orange with black trim scheme in the early to mid-1960s, but this was not officially adopted. In 1971 the WP changed its colors to a dark "Perlman" green with orange lettering. In the course of diesel history, then, the WP had four basic color schemes with additional minor modifications. The final WP colors included a red/orange nose and trim. One Western Pacific locomotive, GP40 3532, was painted in Union Pacific colors with WP lettering after the 1985 merger.

Since the WP was a relatively small railroad, most of the diesel power saw service system-wide. Road engines have been run in three to six unit combinations for over-the-road fast freights. This methodology remained the case ever since the four-unit FTs hit the rails back in the early 1940s. During the 1970s, one could find four units (made up of GP35s or GP40s; or the General Electric U23s or U30s) heading up the fast freight services. Older power like the GP9s were found in switching service, helper service and various way freights. After the *California Zephyr's* last run in March 1970, the passenger power was reassigned to freight services and, in some cases, their steam generators were removed. When operation of the *CZ* behind freight-service U30Bs was considered in the late 1960s, WP purchased three vintage steam generator cars from Great Northern. These also saw passenger extra service. (2)

Chapter 2 Endnotes

1 Western Pacific Railroad Mechanical Records
2 Western Pacific Railroad Mechanical Records

Summary of Western Pacific Diesel Power

Type	Builder	Model	Numbers	Date Built	Remarks
Sw	EMD	SW1	501-503	1939	501 and 502 sold to SN Railway in 1965.
Sw	Alco	S1	504-511	1942	504 sold to SN Ry in1967. 505 and 506 traded to ST&E for NW2s 607 and 608.
Sw	Alco	S2	551-562	1943/1950	562 to SN Ry in 1970.
Sw	Alco	S4	563, 564	1951	
Sw	BLW	VO-1000	581-585	1945	584 to SN Ry in 1970.
Sw	EMD	SW9	601-606	1952	
Sw	EMD	NW2	607, 608	1939/1940	Ex-ST&E 1000 and 1001.
Rd-Sw	EMD	GP7	701-713	1952/1953	711 and 712 to SN Ry in 1971.
Rd-Sw	EMD	GP9	725-732	1955	
Rd-Sw	GE	U30B	751-769	1967/1969	Renumbered 3051-3069 in 1971.
Rd-Sw	GE	U30B	770, 771	1971	Ex-General Electric demonstrators rebuilt to U30Bs in 1971. Renumbered 3070-3071.
Rd-Pass	EMD	F3A	801A, 802A	1947	Regeared for freight and renumbered 925A and 925D.
Rd-Pass	EMD	F3A	803A	1947	
Rd-Pass	EMD	F3A	801D	1948	Ex-NYO&W 503, to WP in 1957 via SN.
Rd-Pass	EMD	F3B	801B, C-803B, C	1947	
Rd-Pass	EMD	FP7A	804A, D-805A, D	1950	
Rd-Pass	EMD	F7B	804B-806B	1950	
Rd-Frt	EMD	FTA	901A, D-912A, D	1941/1944	All retired by 1966.
Rd-Frt	EMD	FTB	901B, C-912B, C	1941/1944	All retired by 1966.
Rd-Frt	EMD	F7A	913A, D-924A, D	1950/1951	
Rd-Frt	EMD	F7B	913B, C-924B, C	1950/1951	
Sw	EMD	SW1500	1501-1503	1973	
Rd-Sw	EMD	GP20	2001-2010	1959/1960	
Rd-Sw	GE	U23B	2251-2265	1972	
Rd-Sw	EMD	GP35	3001-3022	1963/1965	
Rd-Sw	GE	U30B	3051-3071		Renumbered from 751-771 in 1971.
Rd-Sw	EMD	GP40	3501-3544	1966/1971	
Rd-Sw	EMD	GP40-2	3545-3559	1979/1980	

EMD Electro-Motive Division of General Motors
Alco American Locomotive Company
SN Sacramento Northern
NYO&W New York, Ontario & Western
GE General Electric
BLW Baldwin
ST&E Stockton Terminal & Eastern

The next step in switch engine development on the Western Pacific was the 1000 h.p. Alco S2. The 552 is shown here in the then-new solid orange paint scheme in the San Francisco Yard on December 8, 1967. Note the placement of the numberboard above the radiator shutters, which was the standard factory location.

(Collection of the Author)

In the case of the 560, shown here in orange and silver, the numberboard is mounted at an angle on top of the hood. The usual numberboards have been completely blanked out. This unit is laying over between assignments at the engine terminal in Oakland on a "sunny" Sunday afternoon, January 15, 1966.

(Collection of the Author)

The 560 as repainted in the orange scheme, working on the "day" job at Oakland Yard on Monday, December 16, 1968.

(Collection of the Author)

The Western Pacific purchased two 1000 h.p. S4 units, the 563 and 564, from Alco in 1951. This photo shows the 564 in the solid orange color scheme.
(Collection of the Author)

S4 563 received the green paint scheme with orange striping, lettering and numerals. The unit is at the Stockton engine terminal on April 26, 1973.
(Bob Larson)

The Western Pacific did not invest heavily in Baldwins during the diesel age. Indeed, the 585 (shown here at Stockton in March, 1967) was but one of five VO-1000s (581-585) that the company purchased in 1945. They would not have done that, except for the fact that switchers were not immediately available from EMD.
(Collection of the Author)

Baldwin VO-1000 581 in this photo is painted silver and orange. Note the placement of the WP and 581 adjacent to the headlight as well as the application of the front end safety striping. The 581 was photographed before going on duty at the Stockton yard on November 7, 1967.

(J. R. Quinn)

Western Pacific Switcher Paint Schemes

Scheme	Placement	Examples
Solid Black	Black body with white trim and striping; "Western Pacific" in Roman lettering; "Feather River Route" in Gothic.	Alco S1, S2, S4; Baldwin VO-1000; EMD SW1; (SW1 without end striping).
Silver and Orange	Silver body with wide orange band; Black end striping; "Western Pacific" in Gothic.	All switch engines except the SW1500s.
Solid Orange	Orange body; "Western Pacific" in Gothic.	All models except the SW1500s.
Solid "Perlman" Green	Green body; Orange lettering; (Variations with single stripe on front ends of some units – see photographs).	Alco S1 510; all EMDs including the SW1500s.

(top) Side view of SW9 603 in the orange and silver color scheme.

(Bob Larson)

(above) SW9s 601-606 of 1952 were equipped with folding end walkways for multiple-unit operation. 604 is seen at Sacramento on September 9, 1966.

(Collection of the Author)

(left) End stripes were omitted from the orange scheme. However, note the reflective safety strips along the frame of 604 at Sacramento, November 4, 1967.

(Collection of the Author)

(left) The Western Pacific acquired two older NW2s (607 and 608) from the Stockton Terminal and Eastern in 1968. The units were built in 1939 and 1940 for the Union Pacific, which is the "why" for the fat cylindrical stacks. The NW2s came from ST&E as a trade for two WP Alcos, and were rebuilt by the WP with 1200 h.p. engines. They wore solid orange paint right from the beginning of their WP careers. The 608 was photographed in service at Sacramento in May 1969.

(Collection of the Author)

(left) The only WP switch engines to wear the solid green right from the beginning were the SW1500s delivered from EMD in 1973. The 1501 is shown here leading the 1503 at Burlington Northern's Cicero, Illinois, yard en route to the WP.

(Bob Larson)

(below) The GP7 started a motive power trend that has not ended yet. The hood style was originally intended for branch line service, but proved so effective that the units were immediately recognized for their versatility with fast main-line freight and passenger trains. Such is the case with the 701 leading a local freight train at Oakland, California, in 1958.

(Jim Shaw)

Road Switchers

(right) Although sunshine glare obscures the number of GP7 704, this photo shows the application of the black striping at both ends of the GP7 – as applied from the early 1950s to the early 1960s. Portola, California, May 30, 1966.
(Collection of the Author)

(below) Left and right side views of GP7s. Note small road numbers to left of insignia on cab, and one-line placement of roadname.
(Both, J.R. Quinn)

(above) The Western Pacific ran through some rugged snow country and consequently some units, such as the 703 and 706, were equipped with pilot plows salvaged from retired F-units. Portola, California.

(Bob Larson)

(left) There were some modifications to the silver and orange paint scheme as time went on. GP7 708 illustrates the orange nose with a single silver safety stripe. Seen at Oakland on August 8, 1969.

(Collection of the Author)

(left) The rear of GP7 706 illustrates a similar application, but note the curvature of the orange at the top of the unit. Although it is the same application used with the black striping, it looks different without the stripes. The 706 is working the yard at Sacramento on Saturday, May 31, 1969.

(Collection of the Author)

(right) GP7 713 in the modern Perlman green scheme at Chico, California, in 1980.
(Jim Shaw)

GP9s 725 to 732 arrived in 1955. They were equipped with the unique Pyle-National headlight, and in many ways were identical to the GP7s. Different louver placement caused the words "Western Pacific" to be staggered. GP9 726 and GP7 706 were at the Stockton roundhouse on November 7, 1967.
(Collection of the Author)

(below) GP9 726 leads an extra at Norvell, California.
(Bob Larson)

Western Pacific Road Switcher Paint Schemes

Scheme	Placement	Examples
Silver and Orange	Silver body with orange band on side; Orange ends; Black safety stripes on ends; "Western Pacific" in Gothic lettering; Black non-reflective paint on top of low noses.	GP7; GP9; GP20; GP35; GP40; U30B.
Modified Silver and Orange	Same as above except for a single reflective Scotchlite™ stripe on end.	703 and 706.
Solid "Perlman" Green	Green body with orange trim and lettering; "Western Pacific" in Roman lettering. staggered block "WP" or stripes on nose.	702, 727; all GP20; GP35; GP40; U23B; U30B.
	Some GP20s had orange stripes.	2004 and 2005.
Green and Orange	Green body with orange nose and patch on side of cab; Orange pilot or plow. This "new image" scheme included non-staggered "WP" initials on nose.	GP40-2.

Rear end view of GP9 727 showing application of striping and barrel headlight and the overall balance of the orange and silver scheme. Portola, California, June 26, 1966.
(Collection of the Author)

The GP20s continued the tradition of orange and silver with black safety stripes. These 2000 h.p. units, with dual controls, brought the Western Pacific into the world of turbocharged units. The ten GP20s, 2001 to 2010, were also equipped with the traditional Pyle-National barrel headlight. Note that the words "Western Pacific" could be applied on one line, as illustrated with the 2007 at Salt Lake City on August 6, 1965.
(Bob Larson)

(above) The 2010 illustrates the right-hand side of this group of GP20s. Except for Great Northern, Western Pacific was the only other railroad to purchase GP20s with a high short hood. The Great Northern, by the way, utilized the long end as the front end. These units are laying over at Keddie, California, in 1970.

(Bob Larson)

(right) In 1971, the WP adopted the Perlman green color scheme with orange lettering and larger numbers on the cab. Who can miss 2004, and of course larger letters for the words "Western Pacific," which were now applied in the staggered style on the GP20s. Portola, California, 1977

(Bob Larson)

(right) GP20 2005 illustrates the placement of lettering on the left side of the green scheme. Note the placement of the bell on the roof just behind the cab. The 2005 was photographed at Elko, Nevada, in 1976.

(Jim Shaw)

(above) This photo shows the first run of WP's new GP35s at Portola in 1963. WP skipped the EMD GP30 and went right to the GP35. Actually, part of this had to do with the timing of the order and the start of GP35 production. WP purchased 22 of these 2500 h.p. beauties, 3001-3022, in the traditional orange and silver scheme with black stripes. Some customs die hard, though, and the GP35s were equipped with the large bulb style headlight.

(Bob Larson)

(upper left) In the GP35s' early years they carried footboards instead of plows, as on the 3005 at Stockton on December 23, 1967.

(Collection of the Author)

(left) This photo shows the application of the striping at the rear of the GP35s when relatively new in 1965. In this case, the 3017 is MU'd between two F-units.

(Collection of the Author)

(above) The ultimate in styling changes for the WP GP35s came late in the game with a combination green and orange color scheme, changes in the headlight and signal lights in the nose and above the cab, and air-conditioning. The 3009 was photographed on the wye near Kaw Tower in Armstrong Yard, Kansas City, February, 1983.
(Union Pacific Railroad Photo)

(left) 3003 was the only GP35 to receive the all-orange color scheme with black safety stripes. Still the number is barely visible on the side of the cab. Seen at Portola, California, on July 10, 1966
(Bob Larson)

(left)The next-to-last scheme was Perlman green with WP initials and stripes on the nose. The 3010's headlight has been changed to the more customary twin sealed beam. Again note the lack of a plow on the 3010, which also had the distinction of being the first unit with WP initials on the nose. Portola, California, April 8, 1973.
(Bob Larson)

(above) GP40 3512 was repainted from orange and silver to green with single safety stripe and WP initials on the nose. Cab was stenciled "This unit equipped with fuel saver." Salt Lake City, September 1979. *(J. R. Quinn)*

(left) GP40 3541 on symbol freight Second PBF at Blairsden, California, on November 6, 1971, shows the as-delivered appearance of 3527-3544. The signal light in the nose was becoming a WP practice. 3541 became the 1976 for the bicentennial celebration. *(Bob Larson)*

(left) WP purchased 44 GP40s between 1966 and 1971, numbered 3501-3544. The first 16 arrived in silver and orange with black safety stripes, footboards and large headlight. The first new WP units to arrive in green were 3517-3526, in 1970. (3505 had been involved in a wreck and was traded for 3523). The 1970 batch came with twin sealed beam headlights and signal lights in the nose. The last of the group, 3526, at Duluth, Minnesota, had lost its nose signal light by the time of this early 1980s photo. *(Patrick C. Dorin)*

Swinging back to the original part of the GP40 order, these units were extensively refitted with air conditioning, nose signal lights and the new green and orange color scheme. 3502 is seen at Portola, California, in January 1981.

(Bob Larson)

GP40-2s 3545 -3559 were the ultimate WP diesel power during the last days of independent operation. Equipped with air-conditioning, extended range dynamic brakes and several other features, the units wore the final WP scheme of green and orange. Note the lack of pilot plow on the 3553 at Doyle, California, on May 21, 1981.

(Bob Larson)

GP40-2 3558, at Portola, California, in July 1980, illustrates the right side of these units, as well as the pilot plow.

(Bob Larson)

(above) Before completing this section on hood units, we cannot forget General Electric's contribution to WP's motive power roster. The road owned and operated a fleet of 21 U30Bs, numbered 3051 to 3071 (originally 751-771). This photo illustrates 760 with a pilot plow. All of the GEs were so equipped. The original color scheme: orange and silver, of course. These units were purchased between 1967 and 1971. 760 is seen prior to departure from Oakland on August 8, 1969.

(Collection of the Author)

(upper left) U30B 3060, at Portola, California, in May 1973, was the former 760. It should be remarked here that the first five U30Bs, 751 to 755, were actually built in late U28B bodies. Many, if not all, of the U30Bs were repainted in the green scheme, and some of them, like 771, were actually green before renumbering.

(Bob Larson)

(left) 763 leads four units with another GE bringing up the rear, powering a time freight which included both general and intermodal traffic. Salt Lake City, May 1969.

(J. R. Quinn)

SPEED RESTRICTIONS FOR ENGINES: Maximum speed in miles per hour shown below is subject to further restrictions applicable to certain territories as shown in Maximum Speeds:

WESTERN PACIFIC

Class	Unit HP	Engine Maximum Speed	Class	Unit HP	Engine Maximum Speed
805A-804B	1500	65	701-713	1500	65
918-926	1500	65	725-732	1750	65
510	660	35	2001-2010	2000	71
551-564	1000	35	3001-3022	2500	71
559-564			3501-3544	3000	71
in multiple	1000	30	3051-3071	3000	75
581-585	1000	65	2251-2265	2250	75
601-608	1200	30			

Foreign railroad diesel units, when used, will be permitted maximum speeds but will not exceed maximum speed stencilled in cab of each unit.

Trains handling engines dead in train must not exceed the maximum speed for such class engine.

WP diesel locomotive speed table from Consolidated Eastern and Western Division Timetable Number 1, June 11, 1972, p. 29.

(right) U23Bs 2251-2265 arrived in the green scheme and were equipped with dual controls and, like the U30s, EMD Blomberg trucks. The 2250 h.p. units were used in all types of service, including mainline time freights, locals, turns and even switching assignments. 2253 is shown here with orange safety stripes at North Platte, Nebraska, in January 1973. *(J. R. Quinn)*

(below) The last unit of the group, 2265 was stenciled "This unit equipped with fuel saver." Note the mismatched battery box door from an orange and silver U30B. *(J. R. Quinn)*

Covered Wagons

(above) The A-B-B-A FTs on this eastbound February 1944 detour over the SP at Wadsworth, Nevada, show the original WP F-unit scheme of Woodfield green and Diamond yellow with Omaha orange pinstriping. Pilot and underframe were black. As delivered, the FT A- and B-units were semi-permanently coupled – note the wider space between the two B-units in this view.

(Bob Larson)

(left) The original scheme did not last long, as it was too expensive to maintain. One of the next schemes was solid orange with black striping and lettering, as on 903-D at Stockton in February 1950.

(Harold K. Vollrath Collection)

(left) The color scheme that was finally adopted, and retained for most of the careers of the Fs, was the now-classic orange and silver, as on FT 909-D leading this four unit lashup at Portola.

(Bob Larson)

(above) 911-D in orange and silver sports one of the massive plows. Note the large WP insignia at the upper rear of the first B-unit.

(Bob Larson)

(right) The FTs were purchased in four-unit sets with the numbers carrying the suffixes A to D. In this photo the 910-D leads such a set – the customary way of doing things during the early history of this motive power. This long train is at Oakland in 1958 – not an unusual sight at the time.

(J. W. Shaw)

(right) More FTs in action: the 908-D leads a semi-permanently coupled FTB, with an F3 trailing the group on this long freight at Oakland in 1958.

(J. W. Shaw)

(above) FT 905-D shows the latter-day large lettering placement on these units – note the original lettering starting to bleed through. Salt Lake City, January 1964.

(J. R. Quinn)

(left) F3s 801-A and 802-A were equipped with steam generators for use on the *California Zephyr*.

(Collection of the Author)

(left) Boiler-equipped orange and silver F3B 802-B at Salt Lake City in June 1966.

(Bob Larson)

(below) F3 801-A's winged WP nose insignia marked it as a passenger unit.

(J. R. Quinn)

F7s 913-A, D to 924-A, D were built in 1950-51. They were painted orange and silver with small lettering. Note lack of lettering on the B-unit.
(Bob Larson)

Western Pacific F-Unit Paint Schemes

Scheme	Placement	Examples
Green and Yellow	Woodfield Green roof and top section; Diamond Yellow mid-section; Woodfield Green bottom section; Black underframe and pilot; Omaha Orange pinstriping separating yellow and green; small "Western Pacific" in Gothic lettering.	FTs only.
Silver and Orange	Silver sides; Orange nose and side of cab to the door; Black roof, nose top and underbody; Black and white striping on pilot; "Western Pacific" in Gothic lettering.	FTs only, including 902 and 907.
Orange (1940s only)	Orange body with black pinstripes; Black roof nose top and underbody. Orange stripes on pilot; "Western Pacific" in Gothic lettering. (Note: Orange known as International Airport Orange.)	FTs such as 901 and 902.
Orange and Silver	Predominate scheme; Silver lower section (stainless steel on FP7s); Orange nose and mid-section; Silver top section; Black roof (Freight units had black down to the orange nose. Passenger units had the black end at rear of cab area with silver on the cab roof. This black actually ended in a point with sweeping curves, although some passenger units did not have the point); Original "Western Pacific" in black Gothic lettering, later in Roman. Passenger units had winged WP nose insignia, while freight units only had two black stripes on each side.	All F-units.
Solid Orange	Orange body and black roof; "Western Pacific" in black Roman lettering	F7.
Solid "Perlman" Green	Green body with orange striping; Orange "Western Pacific" in Roman lettering Staggered orange block "WP" on the nose.	F7.

(above) F7 914-D in 1968. Nose insignia on freight units was flanked by two black stripes.

(J. R. Quinn)

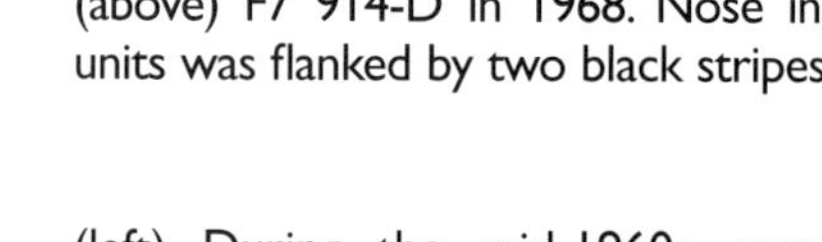

(left) During the mid-1960s, several WP F-units received solid orange paint, and nose m.u. connections. 915-D is shown at Oakland on October 29, 1967.

(Collection of the Author)

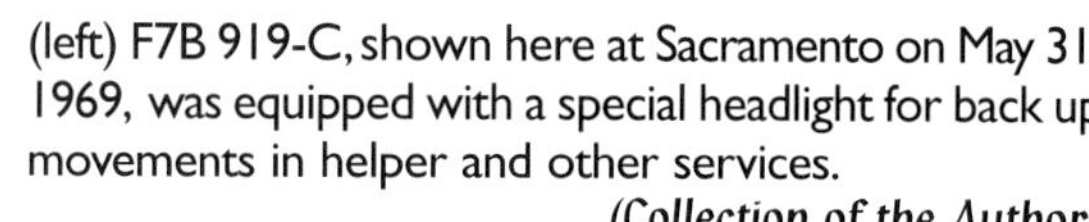

(left) F7B 919-C, shown here at Sacramento on May 31, 1969, was equipped with a special headlight for back up movements in helper and other services.

(Collection of the Author)

(below) The final paint scheme on three of the last four F-units was the green and orange. WP initials graced the nose door with orange striping and lettering on the 917, 918 and 921. Only 913 retained a modified orange and silver scheme. The letter suffixes had been dropped by the end of the 1970s. WP 917 was photographed at North Platte, Nebraska, on the Union Pacific.

(Union Pacific Railroad Photo)

(right) Some of the F7B units carried a Western Pacific insignia on their lower sides, as can be seen in this three-unit lash-up on a time freight at Oakland, California, in 1958.

(Jim Shaw)

(right) Western Pacific FP7As 804-A, D to 805-A, D were purchased for operation on the *California Zephyr*. As passenger units, they were equipped with both a Mars light, and a headlight in the nose door, whereas freight units were only equipped with one headlight. The 805-A shows the orange and silver scheme in March 1969 - just right for the *California Zephyr*.

(J.R. Quinn)

(right and below) FP7s 804-A and 805-D in the Western Pacific's orange and silver scheme were works of art. These FPs were usually MU'd with steam generator-equipped F3Bs in *California Zephyr* service. 804-A is seen at Salt Lake City in October 1968. Note that 805-D has lost its nose wings in this May 1969 view, also at Salt Lake City.

(Both, J.R. Quinn)

3 Passenger Equipment

The Western Pacific operated a wide variety of passenger services for a railroad of its size. Besides the superb domeliner *California Zephyr* (operated jointly with Burlington and Rio Grande), the company operated both local passenger train services as well as secondary mainline standard trains. WP also operated a pair of *Zephyrettes*, one of the longest runs using Budd Company Rail Diesel Cars. Consequently, the WP owned and operated both standard and streamlined passenger equipment as well as self-contained cars, in a wide range of configurations from the head-end to the rear-end including a fleet of business cars. Suburban or commuter trains were the only passenger service not offered by the WP, and as this is being written in 1997 such service is being considered for the San Francisco-Oakland area over former WP tracks.

It is the purpose of this chapter to explore the range of passenger equipment operated by the WP throughout its history, from 1909 until its inclusion in the Union Pacific in the mid-1980s. The following photos, diagrams, and rosters will provide modelers with useful information for the creation of Western Pacific passenger trains, as well as provide pleasant memories of WP passenger travel.

(facing page) Mention passenger trains on the Western Pacific and the *California Zephyr* seems to pop up first. Here the *CZ* is in the Feather River Canyon early in its career behind F3 803.
(Rail Photo Service)

(right) WP purchased three Great Northern steam generator cars for use with either aging Fs or GE U-boats and late-model EMDs on the *CZ* and passenger extras. Car 593 is former GN 6, and was at Stockton in 1969.
(Bob Larson)

(right) Heater car 591, also ex-GN. Stockton, California, February 14, 1970
(Collection of Howard W. Ameling)

(left) The *CZ* at Stockton in 1969 with a heater car on the head-end.
(Collection of Howard W. Ameling)

(left) WP converted tenders from three ex-Florida East Coast 4-8-2s into fuel and water cars to run behind passenger diesels handling either secondary schedules or extras, to eliminate fuel and water stops. In silver and orange, 852 and 853 were at Oakland in 1956.
(Bob Larson)

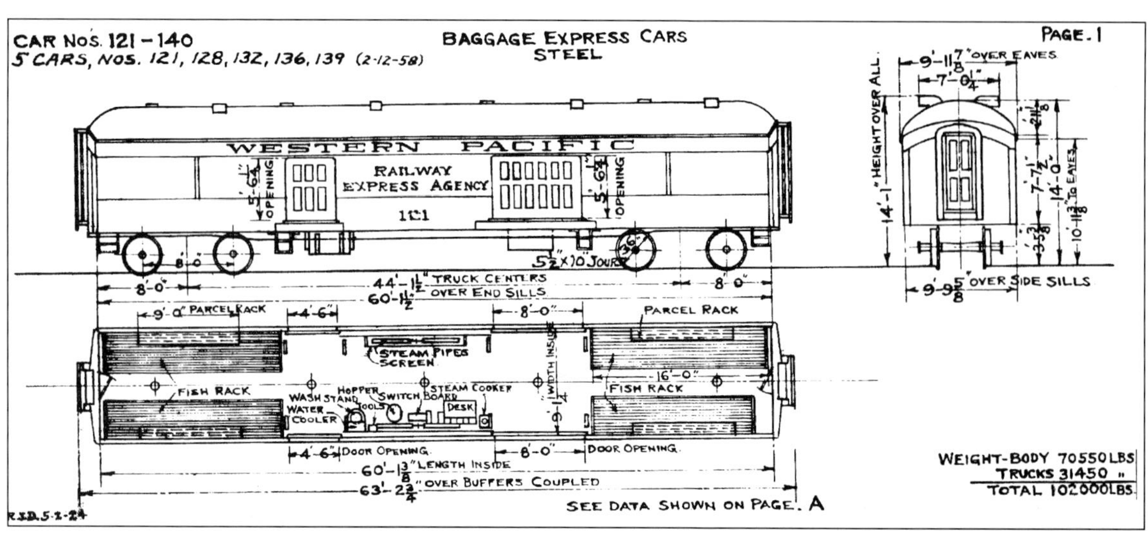

(right) WP's box express cars are something of a mystery. They were 40-foot cars, painted green with gold lettering and a WP insignia to the right of the door. Car 22085 is on the head end of train 1 at Alvarado Junction in 1946.

(Collection of Bob Larson)

The backbone of the Western Pacific baggage car fleet were 20 of these 60-foot, double door cars. They were painted Pullman green with gold lettering, as on 128 (series 121-140) on display at Oakland, California.

(Collection of Howard W. Ameling)

Western Pacific Heavyweight Passenger Equipment

Configuration	Number	Remarks
Baggage	121-140	Arch roof
Baggage-Railway Post Office	201-205	30' RPO section
Express Refrigerator	250-274	
Express Box	22085	40' long, 6-foot door. Pullman green with gold lettering.
Coach	301-320	84 seats
Cafe-Coach	391-394	40 coach seats/18 dining seats.
Dining Car	501-508	36 seats
Lounge-Observation	651-653	653 named *Feather River.*
Instruction Car	110	
Business Cars	1	
	101	
	105	
	106	

Note: This is a representative list of WP heavyweight equipment in use during the 1940s and 1950s, rather than a comprehensive roster.

(right) Wooden combine 402 was a car for all tasks. In June 1947, when this photo was taken, it was assigned to the B&L local as coach, baggage-express car and caboose. It was indeed an historical piece of equipment, still seeing regular service. The window layout was the same on both sides.
(Collection of Bob Larson)

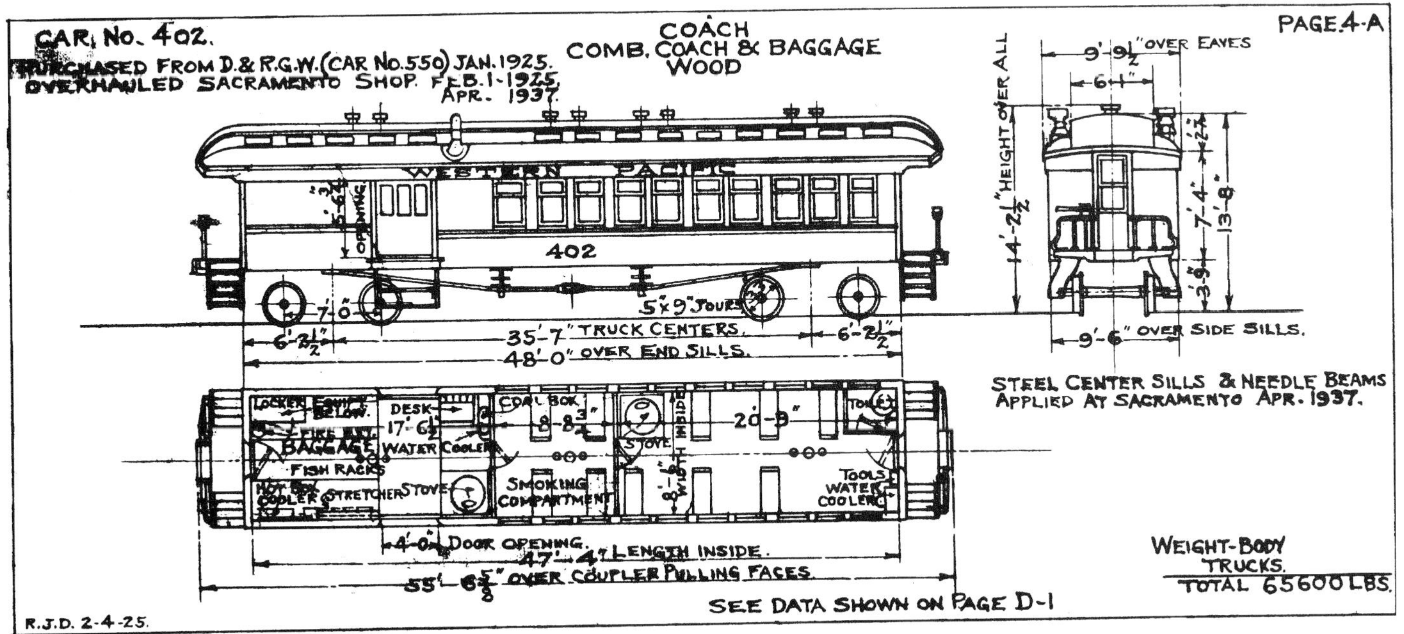

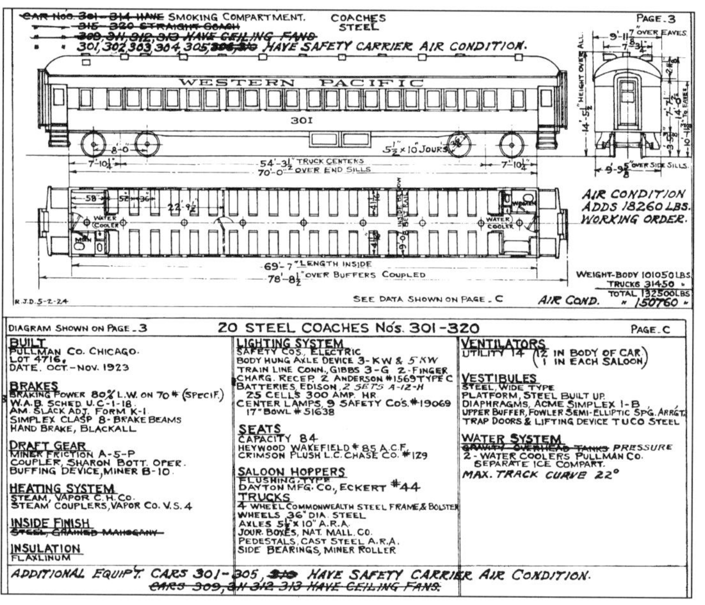
CAR NOS 301-314 HAVE SMOKING COMPARTMENT. COACHES STEEL
315-320 STRAIGHT COACH
300, 311, 312, 313 HAVE CEILING FANS
301, 302, 303, 304, 305, 306, 310 HAVE SAFETY CARRIER AIR CONDITION.
PAGE. 3
WESTERN PACIFIC
301
AIR CONDITION ADDS 18260 LBS. WORKING ORDER.
WEIGHT-BODY 101050 LBS. TRUCKS 31450 " TOTAL 132500 LBS. " 150760 "
R.J.D. 5-2-24
SEE DATA SHOWN ON PAGE. C AIR COND.

DIAGRAM SHOWN ON PAGE. 3 — 20 STEEL COACHES Nos. 301-320 — PAGE. C

BUILT PULLMAN CO. CHICAGO. LOT 4716. DATE. OCT.-NOV. 1923
BRAKES BRAKING POWER 80% L.W. ON 70# (SPECIF.) W.A.B. SCHED. U.C-1-18. AM. SLACK ADJ. FORM K-1. SIMPLEX CLASP 8-BRAKE BEAMS. HAND BRAKE, BLACKALL
DRAFT GEAR MINER FRICTION A-5-P. COUPLER, SHARON BOTT. OPER. BUFFING DEVICE, MINER B-10.
HEATING SYSTEM STEAM, VAPOR C.H. CO. STEAM COUPLERS, VAPOR CO. V.S. 4
INSIDE FINISH STEEL, GRAINED MAHOGANY
INSULATION FLAXLINUM
LIGHTING SYSTEM SAFETY CO'S. ELECTRIC. BODY HUNG AXLE DEVICE 3-KW & 5KW. TRAIN LINE CONN., GIBBS 3-G 2-FINGER. CHARG. RECEP. 2 ANDERSON #1569 TYPE C. BATTERIES, EDISON 2 SETS A-12-H. 25 CELLS 300 AMP. HR. CENTER LAMPS 9 SAFETY CO'S. #19069 17" BOWL #51638
SEATS CAPACITY 84. HEYWOOD WAKEFIELD # 85 A.C.F. CRIMSON PLUSH L.C. CHASE CO. # 129
SALOON HOPPERS FLUSHING TYPE. DAYTON MFG. CO., ECKERT #44
TRUCKS 4 WHEEL COMMONWEALTH STEEL FRAME & BOLSTER. WHEELS 36" DIA. STEEL. AXLES 5½"x10" A.R.A. JOUR. BOXES, NAT. MALL. CO. PEDESTALS, CAST STEEL A.R.A. SIDE BEARINGS, MINER ROLLER
VENTILATORS UTILITY 14 (12 IN BODY OF CAR, 1 IN EACH SALOON)
VESTIBULES STEEL, WIDE TYPE. PLATFORM, STEEL BUILT UP. DIAPHRAGMS, ACME SIMPLEX 1-B. UPPER BUFFER, FOWLER SEMI-ELLIPTIC SPG. ARRGT. TRAP DOORS & LIFTING DEVICE TUCO STEEL
WATER SYSTEM GRAVITY - OVERHEAD TANKS PRESSURE. 2 - WATER COOLERS PULLMAN CO. SEPARATE ICE COMPART.
MAX. TRACK CURVE 22°

ADDITIONAL EQUIP'T. CARS 301-305, 310 HAVE SAFETY CARRIER AIR CONDITION. CARS 309, 311, 312, 313 HAVE CEILING FANS.

(top)The 300-series 84-seat standard coaches rode on four-wheel trucks and were painted Pullman green with gold lettering. Coach 302 is seen on display at Oakland, California.

(Collection of Howard W. Ameling)

(above) Coach 301 was photographed at Oakland in 1957 in a Shriners' Special – as part of the celebration, the car was rather distressingly chalked and painted up.

(Bob Larson)

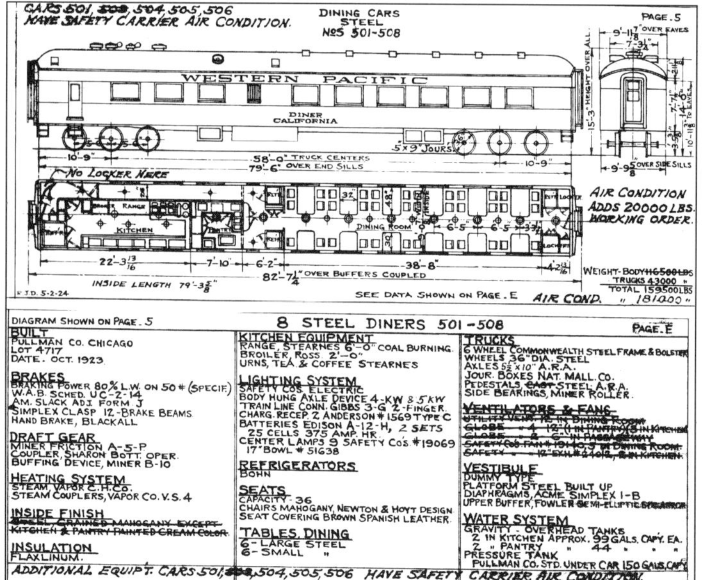
CARS 501, 503, 504, 505, 506 HAVE SAFETY CARRIER AIR CONDITION.
DINING CARS STEEL Nos 501-508
PAGE. 5
WESTERN PACIFIC
DINER CALIFORNIA
NO LOCKER HERE
AIR CONDITION ADDS 20000 LBS. WORKING ORDER.
WEIGHT-BODY 165 LBS. TRUCKS 43000 " TOTAL LBS. " 181000 "
R.J.D. 5-2-24
SEE DATA SHOWN ON PAGE. E AIR COND.

DIAGRAM SHOWN ON PAGE. 5 — 8 STEEL DINERS 501-508 — PAGE. E

BUILT PULLMAN CO. CHICAGO. LOT 4717. DATE. OCT. 1923
BRAKES BRAKING POWER 80% L.W. ON 50# (SPECIF.) W.A.B. SCHED. UC-2-14. AM. SLACK ADJ. FORM J. SIMPLEX CLASP 12-BRAKE BEAMS. HAND BRAKE, BLACKALL
DRAFT GEAR MINER FRICTION A-5-P. COUPLER, SHARON BOTT. OPER. BUFFING DEVICE, MINER B-10
HEATING SYSTEM STEAM, VAPOR C.H. CO. STEAM COUPLERS, VAPOR CO. V.S. 4
INSIDE FINISH STEEL, GRAINED MAHOGANY EXCEPT KITCHEN & PANTRY PAINTED CREAM COLOR.
INSULATION FLAXLINUM.
KITCHEN EQUIPMENT RANGE, STEARNES 6'-0" COAL BURNING. URNS, TEA & COFFEE STEARNES
LIGHTING SYSTEM SAFETY CO'S. ELECTRIC. BODY HUNG AXLE DEVICE 4-KW & 5KW. TRAIN LINE CONN. GIBBS 3-G 2-FINGER. CHARG. RECEP. 2 ANDERSON #1569 TYPE C. BATTERIES EDISON A-12-H, 2 SETS. 25 CELLS 375 AMP. HR. CENTER LAMPS 9 SAFETY CO'S #19069. 17" BOWL # 51638
REFRIGERATORS BOHN
SEATS CAPACITY 36. CHAIRS MAHOGANY, NEWTON & HOYT DESIGN. SEAT COVERING BROWN SPANISH LEATHER.
TABLES, DINING 6 - LARGE STEEL. 6 - SMALL
TRUCKS 6 WHEEL COMMONWEALTH STEEL FRAME & BOLSTER. WHEELS 36" DIA. STEEL. JOUR. BOXES NAT. MALL. CO. PEDESTALS, CAST STEEL A.R.A. SIDE BEARINGS, MINER ROLLER.
VENTILATORS & FANS
VESTIBULE DUMMY TYPE. PLATFORM STEEL BUILT UP. DIAPHRAGMS, ACME SIMPLEX 1-B. UPPER BUFFER, FOWLER SEMI-ELLIPTIC SPG. ARRGT.
WATER SYSTEM GRAVITY - OVERHEAD TANKS. 2 IN KITCHEN APPROX. 99 GALS. CAP'Y. EA. 2 " PANTRY " 44 " " ". PRESSURE TANK PULLMAN CO. STD. UNDER CAR 150 GALS. CAP'Y.

ADDITIONAL EQUIP'T. CARS 501, 503, 504, 505, 506 HAVE SAFETY CARRIER AIR CONDITION.

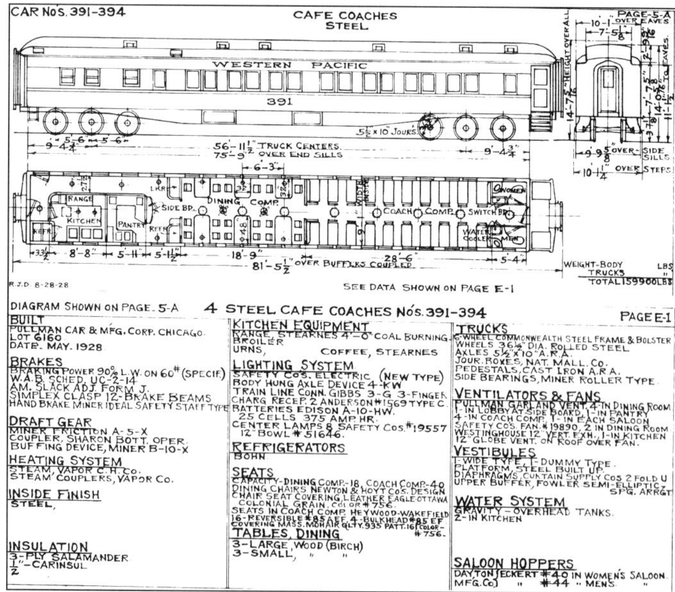
CAR NOS. 391-394 — CAFE COACHES STEEL — PAGE-5-A
WESTERN PACIFIC
391
R.J.D. 8-28-28
WEIGHT-BODY LBS. TRUCKS " TOTAL 159900 LBS.
SEE DATA SHOWN ON PAGE E-1

DIAGRAM SHOWN ON PAGE. 5-A — 4 STEEL CAFE COACHES Nos. 391-394 — PAGE E-1

BUILT PULLMAN CAR & MFG. CORP. CHICAGO. LOT 6160. DATE. MAY. 1928
BRAKES BRAKING POWER 90% L.W. ON 60# (SPECIF) W.A.B. SCHED. UC-2-14. AM. SLACK ADJ. FORM J. SIMPLEX CLASP 12-BRAKE BEAMS. HAND BRAKE MINER IDEAL SAFETY STAFF TYPE
DRAFT GEAR MINER FRICTION A-5-X. COUPLER, SHARON BOTT. OPER. BUFFING DEVICE, MINER B-10-X
HEATING SYSTEM STEAM, VAPOR C.H. CO. STEAM COUPLERS, VAPOR CO.
INSIDE FINISH STEEL
INSULATION 3-PLY SALAMANDER. 1" - CARINSUL.
KITCHEN EQUIPMENT RANGE, STEARNES 4'-0" COAL BURNING. BROILER. URNS, COFFEE, STEARNES
LIGHTING SYSTEM SAFETY CO'S. ELECTRIC (NEW TYPE). BODY HUNG AXLE DEVICE 4-KW. TRAIN LINE CONN. GIBBS 3-G 3-FINGER. CHARG. RECEP. 2 ANDERSON #1569 TYPE C. BATTERIES EDISON A-10-HW. 25 CELLS 375 AMP. HR. CENTER LAMPS 8 SAFETY CO'S. #19557. 12" BOWL #51646.
REFRIGERATORS BOHN
SEATS CAPACITY-DINING COMP.-18, COACH COMP.-46. DINING CHAIRS NEWTON & HOYT CO'S. DESIGN. CHAIR SEAT COVERING LEATHER EAGLE OTTAWA COLONIAL GRAIN, COLOR #756. SEATS IN COACH COMP. HEYWOOD-WAKEFIELD 16-REVERSIBLE #85 A.C.F. & 2-BULKHEAD #85 E.F. COVERING MASS. MOHAIR QLTY. 935 PATT. 16 COLOR #756.
TABLES, DINING 3-LARGE, WOOD (BIRCH). 3-SMALL, " "
TRUCKS 6 WHEEL COMMONWEALTH STEEL FRAME & BOLSTER. WHEELS 36½" DIA. ROLLED STEEL. AXLES 5½"x10" A.R.A. JOUR. BOXES, NAT. MALL. CO. PEDESTALS, CAST IRON A.R.A. SIDE BEARINGS, MINER ROLLER TYPE
VENTILATORS & FANS PULLMAN GARLAND VENT. 4 IN DINING ROOM, 1 IN LOBBY AT SIDE BOARD, 1 IN PANTRY, 4 IN COACH COMP., 1 IN EACH SALOON. SAFETY CO'S. FAN #19890, 2 IN DINING ROOM. WESTINGHOUSE 12" VERT. EXH., 1 IN KITCHEN. 12" GLOBE VENT. ON ROOF OVER FAN.
VESTIBULES WIDE TYPE, 1-DUMMY TYPE. PLATFORM, STEEL BUILT UP. DIAPHRAGMS, CURTAIN SUPPLY CO'S 2 FOLD U. UPPER BUFFER, FOWLER SEMI-ELLIPTIC SPG. ARRGT.
WATER SYSTEM GRAVITY - OVERHEAD TANKS. 2-IN KITCHEN
SALOON HOPPERS DAYTON, ECKERT #40 IN WOMEN'S SALOON. MFG. CO. " #44 " MEN'S "

WP's observation lounge cars (651, 652 and 653) were all equipped with a mini-open-platform at the rear of the sun room. The cars were built by Pullman. Car 653, *Feather River*, is seen at Rio Vista Junction, California, in 1970.

(Bob Larson)

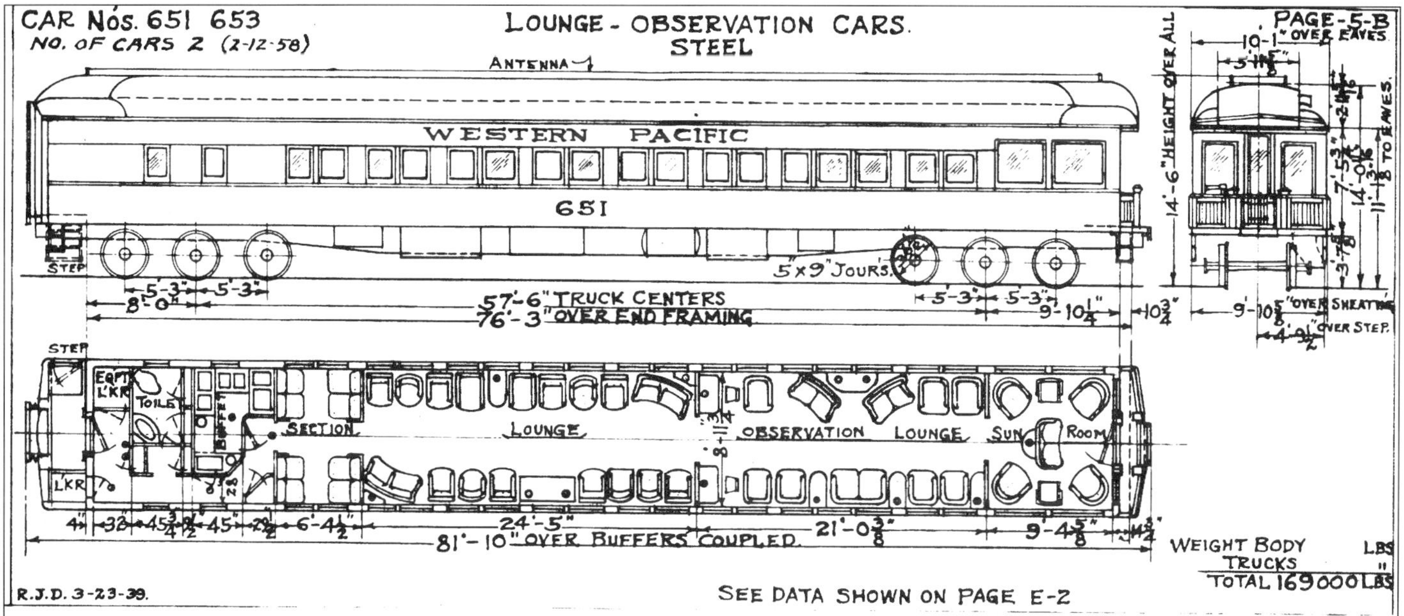

CAR NÓS. 651 653
NO. OF CARS 2 (2-12-58)

LOUNGE - OBSERVATION CARS.
STEEL

PAGE-5-B

ANTENNA
WESTERN PACIFIC
651
STEP
5'x9" JOURS.
5'-3" 5'-3"
8'-0"
57'-6" TRUCK CENTERS
76'-3" OVER END FRAMING
5'-3" 5'-3" 9'-10¼" 10¾"
14'-6" HEIGHT OVER ALL
10'-1" OVER EAVES
11'-8" TO EAVES
9'-10⅝" OVER SHEATHING
4'-9½" OVER STEP

STEP
EQPT. L'KR.
TOILET
BUFFET
SECTION
LOUNGE
OBSERVATION LOUNGE
SUN ROOM
LKR.
4" 32" 45½" 45" 2½" 6'-4½" 24'-5" 21'-0⅜" 9'-4⅝"
81'-10" OVER BUFFERS COUPLED.

WEIGHT BODY LBS
TRUCKS "
TOTAL 169000 LBS

R.J.D. 3-23-39.

SEE DATA SHOWN ON PAGE E-2

DIAGRAM SHOWN ON PAGE-5-B 3-STEEL LOUNGE-OBSERVATION CARS NÓS. 651-653 PAGE-E-2

BUILT
PULLMAN CAR & MFG. CORP. CHICAGO.
LOT NO.
DATE MAY 1931

BRAKES
BRAKING POWER 90% L.W. ON 60# SPECIF.
W.A.B. SCHED. U.C.B.C. 1-18.
AM. SLACK ADJ. TYPE K.
SIMPLEX CLASP BEAMS 12, SPEC. AT DRIVE END
HAND BRAKE-LINDSTOM, VEST. END MALL. IRON ENA.
OBSER. END IMPROVED TYPE WITH DROP HANDLE

DRAFT GEAR
WESTINGHOUSE N-10-F
COUPLER, PASSENGER TYPE "D", BOTT. OPERATING.
BUFFING DEVICE, MINER

HEATING SYSTEM
STEAM, VAPOR C.H. CO.
STEAM COUPLERS, VAPOR CO.

INSIDE FINISH
STEEL, PAINTED SOLID COLORS THROUGHOUT

INSULATION
FLOOR INSULATION, 1" HAIR FELT
SIDES, ENDS, & ROOF SALAMANDER.

BUFFET EQUIPMENT
BROILER WITH MONEL HOOD & LINING
ICE CREAM CHEST, 2 SYPHON BOTTLES
EDLUND CAN OPENER, COFFEE URN, PARKER
HAND COFFEE MILL, ELECTRIC TOASTER, MIXER

LIGHTING SYSTEM
SAFETY COS. ELECTRIC 30 VOLT D.C. FF-D-10, 100 AMP.HR.
GENERATOR, AXLE DEVICE, BODY HUNG #2 SUSPENSION
TRAIN LINE CONN. GIBBS 3-G, 2-FINGER.
CHARG. RECEP. 2 ANDERSON # 1569 TYPE C.
BATTERIES, 2 SETS EDISON A-12-H
50 CELLS 375 AMP. HR
SEE SPECIF. FOR INDIVIDUAL LIGHTING FIXTURE REF.

REFRIGERATOR
IN BUFFET ICED FROM ROOF

SEATS
CAPACITY - LOUNGE-27, OBSERVATION LOUNGE-13
SUN ROOM - 8
SEE SPECIF. FOR INDIVIDUAL CHAIR & SETTEE NO'S

TABLES (PULLMAN)
SUN ROOM-1
OBSERVATION LOUNGE-6
LOUNGE-4
SEE SPECIF. FOR INDIVIDUAL TABLE NO'S.

TRUCKS
6-WHEEL PULLMAN CAST STEEL FRAME & BOLSTER
WHEELS 36½" DIA. ROLLED STEEL
AXLES 5"x9" STEEL A.A.R.
JOUR. BOXES, PULLMANITE
PEDESTALS, BUILT-UP STEEL
SIDE BEARINGS WOODS #310-M.

VENTILATORS & FANS
PULLMAN STANDARD EXHAUST.
3-12" BLOW FANS

AIR CONDITIONING SYSTEM
~~CARS EQUIPPED WITH PULLMAN MECHANICAL SYSTEM WITH AUXILIARY HOLDOVER.~~ WAUKESHA

VESTIBULES
PULLMAN STANDARD STEEL U-BEAM CONSTR.
WITH CANVAS DIAPHRAGM.
OBSERVATION END - CLIPPER TYPE.

WATER SYSTEM.
PULLMAN STANDARD AIR PRESSURE
GALVAN. STEEL TANK & CASING

SALOON HOPPER
DUNER - OPEN TYPE.

Business Cars

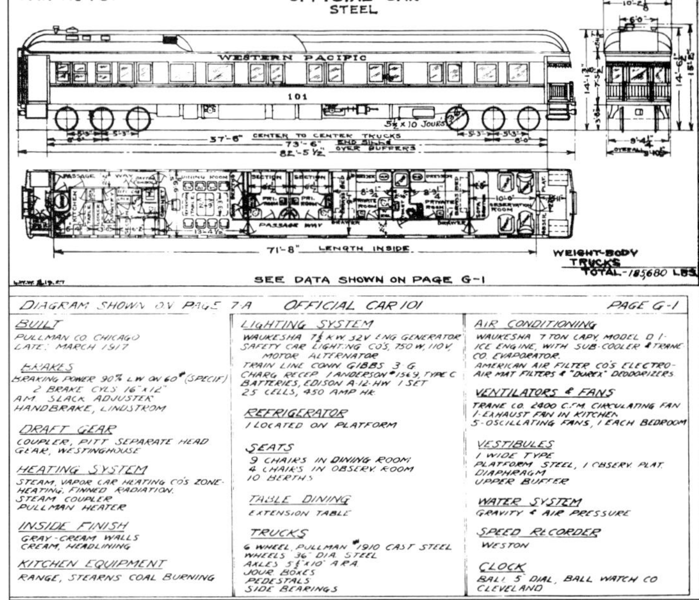

CAR No. 101

OFFICIAL CAR
STEEL

PAGE 7-A

WEIGHT-BODY
TRUCKS
TOTAL-185,680 LBS.

SEE DATA SHOWN ON PAGE G-1

DIAGRAM SHOWN ON PAGE 7-A — OFFICIAL CAR 101 — PAGE G-1

BUILT
PULLMAN CO. CHICAGO
DATE: MARCH 1917

BRAKES
BRAKING POWER 90% LW ON 60# (SPECIF)
2 BRAKE CYLS 16"x12"
AM. SLACK ADJUSTER
HANDBRAKE, LINDSTROM

DRAFT GEAR
COUPLER, PITT SEPARATE HEAD
GEAR, WESTINGHOUSE

HEATING SYSTEM
STEAM, VAPOR CAR HEATING CO'S ZONE-HEATING, FINNED RADIATION.
STEAM COUPLER
PULLMAN HEATER

INSIDE FINISH
GRAY-CREAM WALLS
CREAM, HEADLINING

KITCHEN EQUIPMENT
RANGE, STEARNS COAL BURNING

LIGHTING SYSTEM
WAUKESHA 7½ KW 32V ENG GENERATOR
SAFETY CAR LIGHTING CO'S, 750 W, 110 V, MOTOR ALTERNATOR
TRAIN LINE CONN. GIBBS 3-G
CHARG RECEP. 1 ANDERSON #1569, TYPE C
BATTERIES, EDISON A-12-HW 1 SET
25 CELLS, 450 AMP HR

REFRIGERATOR
1 LOCATED ON PLATFORM

SEATS
9 CHAIRS IN DINING ROOM
4 CHAIRS IN OBSERV. ROOM
10 BERTHS

TABLE DINING
EXTENSION TABLE

TRUCKS
6 WHEEL, PULLMAN #1910 CAST STEEL
WHEELS 36" DIA. STEEL
AXLES 5½"x10" A.R.A.
JOUR. BOXES
PEDESTALS
SIDE BEARINGS

AIR CONDITIONING
WAUKESHA 7 TON CAPY, MODEL D1-ICE ENGINE, WITH SUB-COOLER & TRANE CO. EVAPORATOR.
AMERICAN AIR FILTER CO'S ELECTRO-AIR MAT FILTERS & "DUREX" DEODORIZERS

VENTILATORS & FANS
TRANE CO. 2400 C.F.M. CIRCULATING FAN
1-EXHAUST FAN IN KITCHEN
5-OSCILLATING FANS, 1 EACH BEDROOM

VESTIBULES
1 WIDE TYPE
PLATFORM STEEL, 1 OBSERV. PLAT.
DIAPHRAGM
UPPER BUFFER

WATER SYSTEM
GRAVITY & AIR PRESSURE

SPEED RECORDER
WESTON

CLOCK
BALL 5" DIAL, BALL WATCH CO
CLEVELAND

(top) WP Business Car 101 wears a very attractive green and orange scheme at Salt Lake City in July 1966.

(Bob Larson)

(above) Car 101 was originally painted in the "usual" Pullman Green with gold lettering. In this 1957 photo at Oakland, the car has been decorated by the Shriners for the same Circus Train that included coach 301 shown on page 60.

(Bob Larson)

(right) The scheme was eventually modified to a set of four stripes, as shown at Oroville in June 1972.

(Bob Larson)

(left) The right side of Business Car 101, at Oakland, California, in March 1975.

(Bob Larson)

(above) Business Car 1 was painted green with orange striping. Oroville, June 1972.

(Bob Larson)

(right) WP cars 101 and 1 at Oroville in June 1972. Car 1 was purchased in 1971, and was the last WP Business Car in operation through the 1970s.

(Bob Larson)

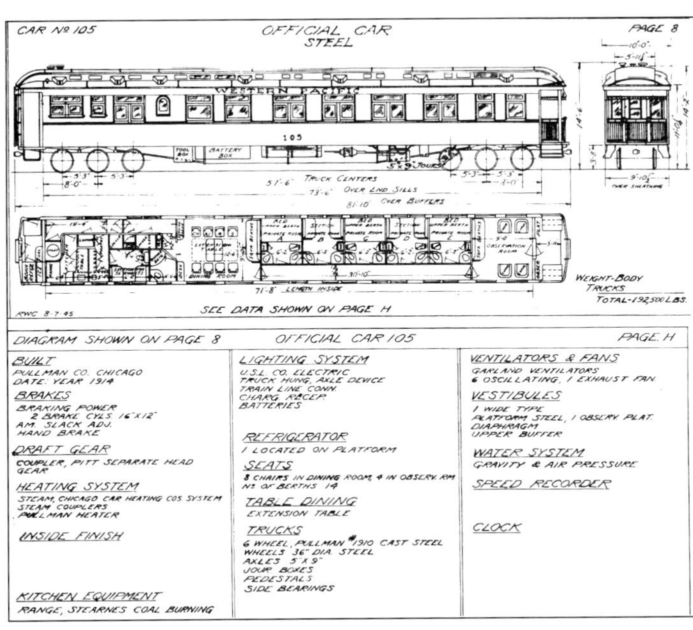

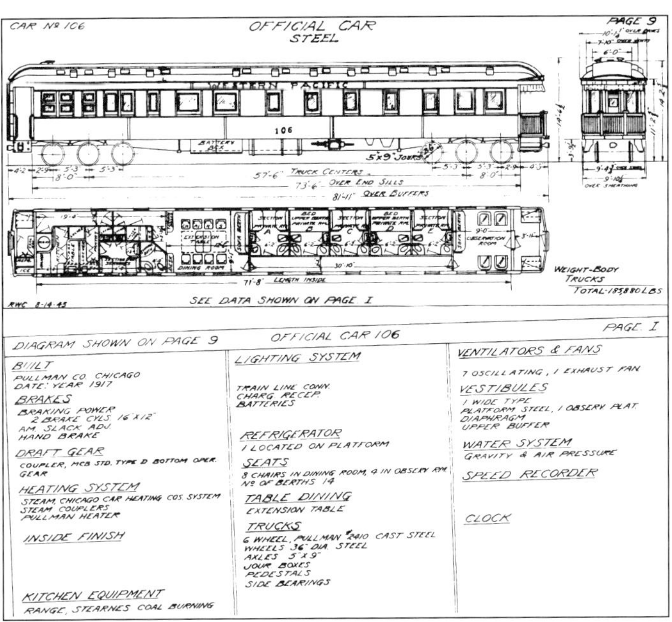

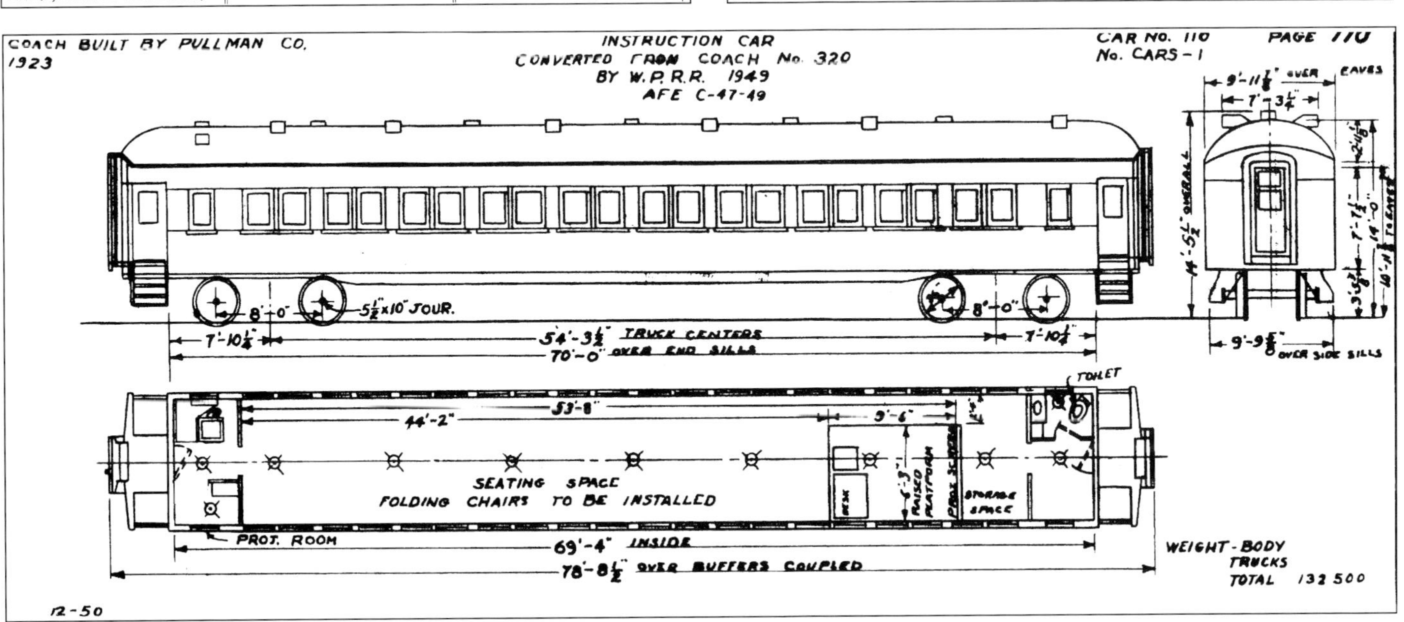

THE VISTA DOME *California Zephyr*

The *CZ* was a true streamliner, and each train had one baggage car that was a perfect match. WP's *Silver Beaver* illustrates this concept complete to its skirting. Oakland, May 30, 1948.

(Bob Larson)

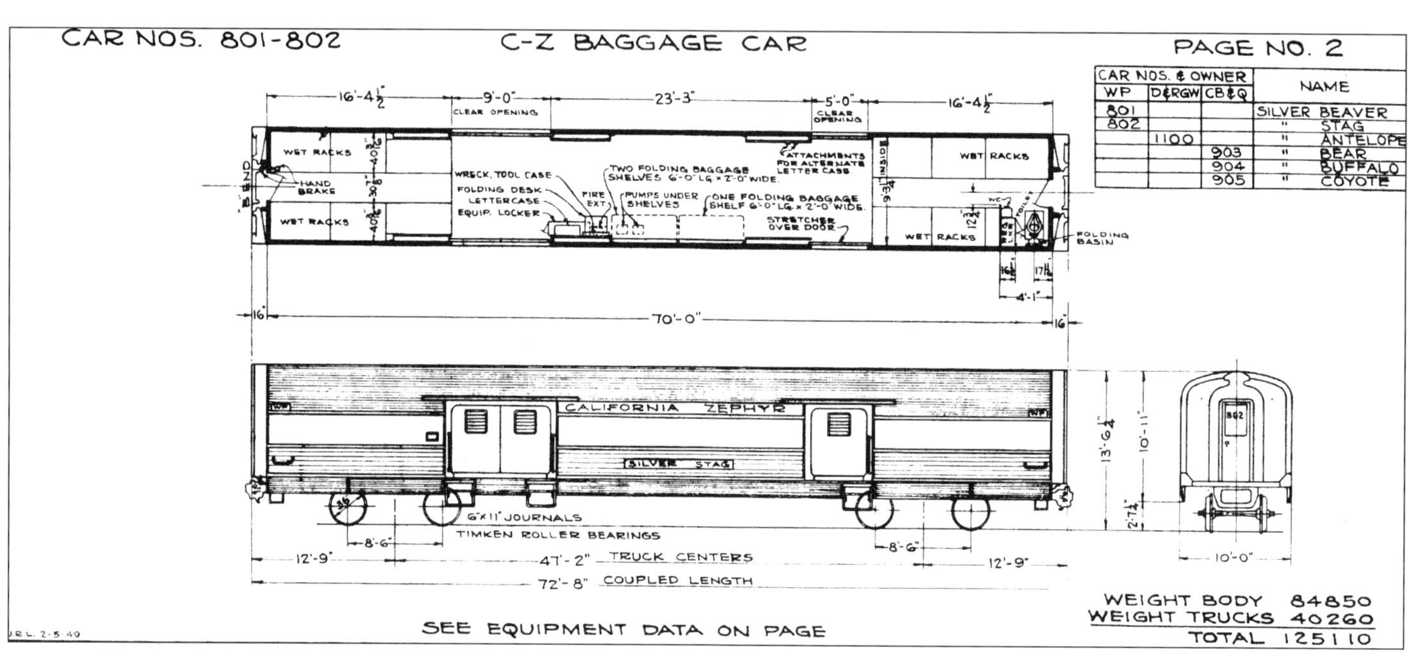

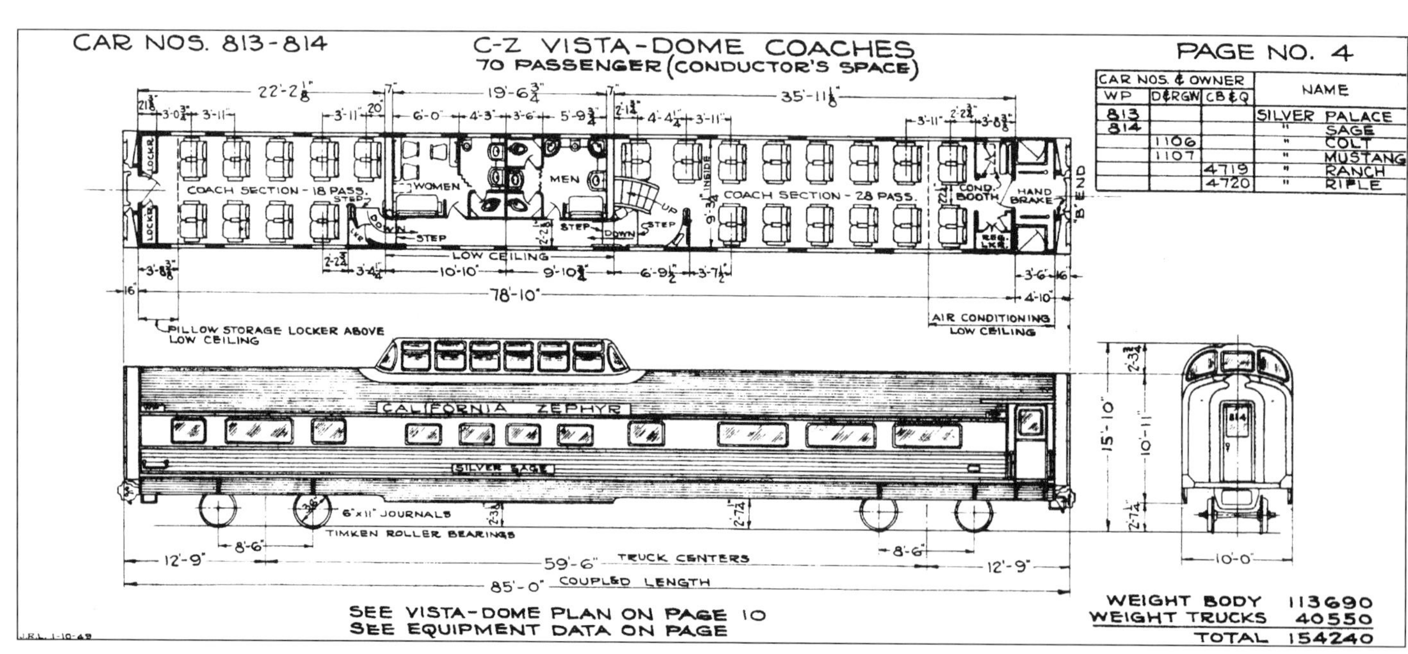

WP dome coach *Silver Sage* contained a Conductor's office (window next to vestibule).

(Harold K. Vollrath Collection)

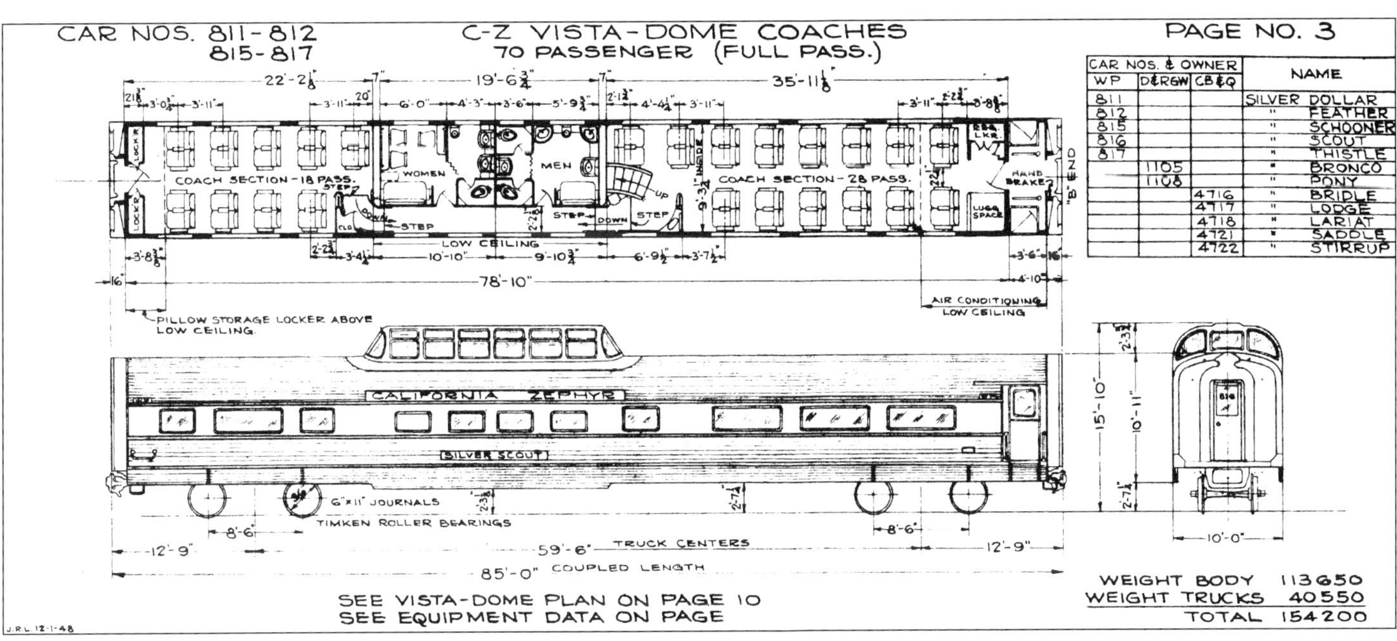

CAR NOS. & OWNER			NAME
WP	D&RGW	CB&Q	
811			SILVER DOLLAR
812			" FEATHER
815			" SCHOONER
816			" SCOUT
817			" THISTLE
	1105		" BRONCO
	1108		" PONY
		4716	" BRIDLE
		4717	" LODGE
		4718	" LARIAT
		4721	" SADDLE
		4722	" STIRRUP

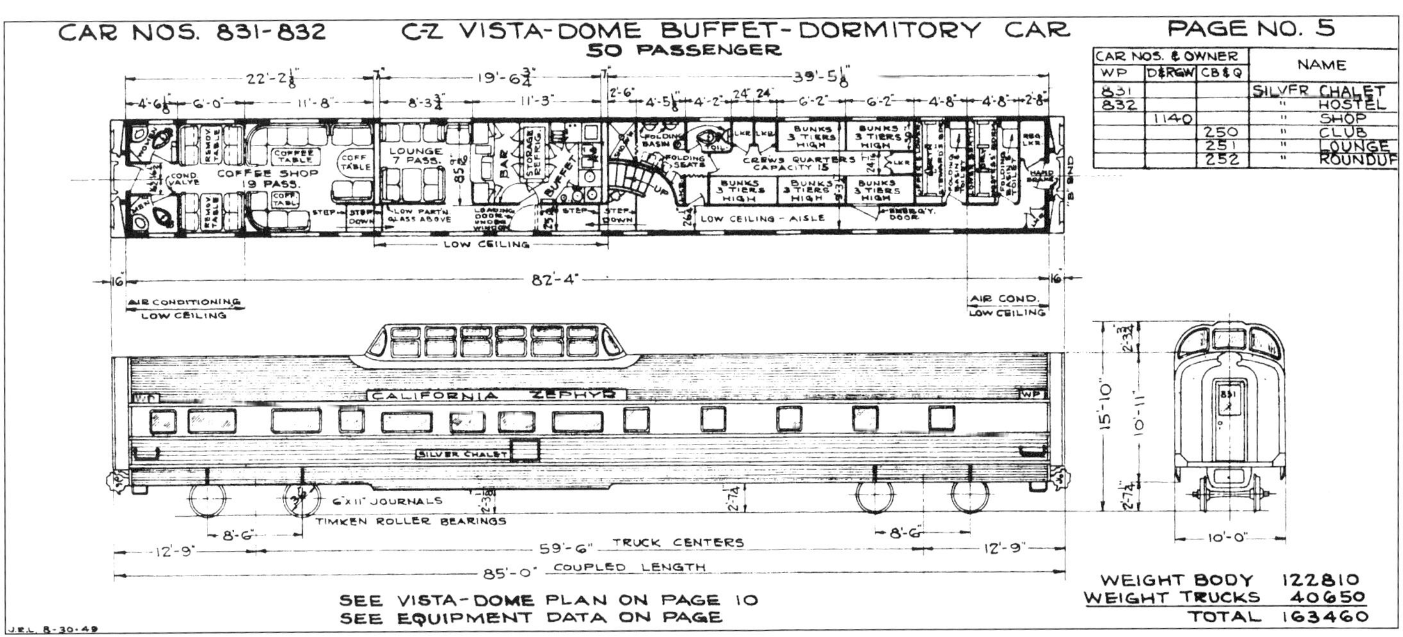

CAR NOS. & OWNER			NAME
WP	D&RGW	CB&Q	
831			SILVER CHALET
832			" HOSTEL
	1140		" SHOP
		250	" CLUB
		251	" LOUNGE
		252	" ROUNDUP

(above) All WP dome coaches were not alike. *Silver Feather* was a "full passenger," without a Conductor's office. Western Pacific's *CZ* cars were identified by the "WP" at each upper corner.

(Budd Company, Author's Collection)

(left) WP *Silver Dollar* shows the left-hand side of both types of dome coaches (the vestibule is at the rear). By the time of this March 22, 1970, view at Portola, for safety and maintenance reasons the wide diaphragms were removed and each car sported a small number just below its WP initials, next to the vestibule.

(Bob Larson)

(left) WP *Silver Bay* was a ten roomette-six double bedroom sleeper. The vestibule was at the front of these cars.

(Budd Company, Author's Collection)

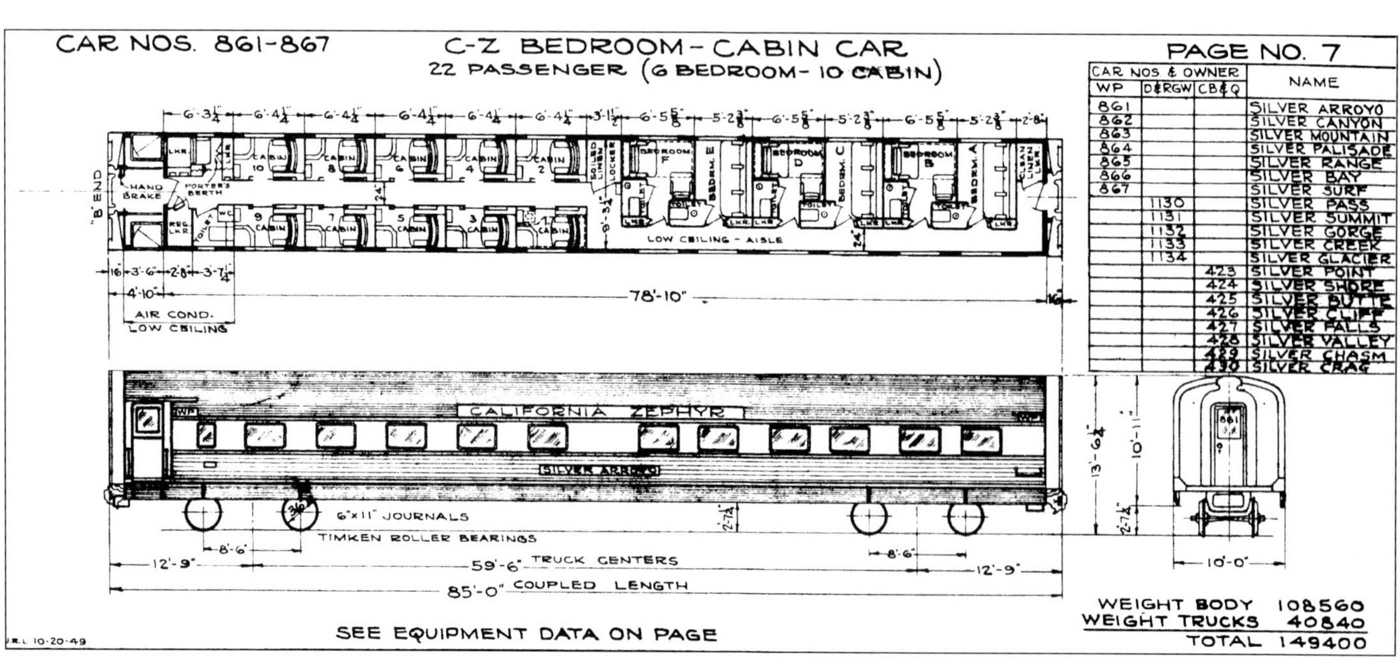

CAR NOS. & OWNER			NAME
WP	D&RGW	CB&Q	
861			SILVER ARROYO
862			SILVER CANYON
863			SILVER MOUNTAIN
864			SILVER PALISADE
865			SILVER RANGE
866			SILVER BAY
867			SILVER SURF
	1130		SILVER PASS
	1131		SILVER SUMMIT
	1132		SILVER GORGE
	1133		SILVER CREEK
	1134		SILVER GLACIER
		423	SILVER POINT
		424	SILVER SHORE
		425	SILVER BUTTE
		426	SILVER CLIFF
		427	SILVER FALLS
		428	SILVER VALLEY
		429	SILVER CHASM
		430	SILVER CRAG

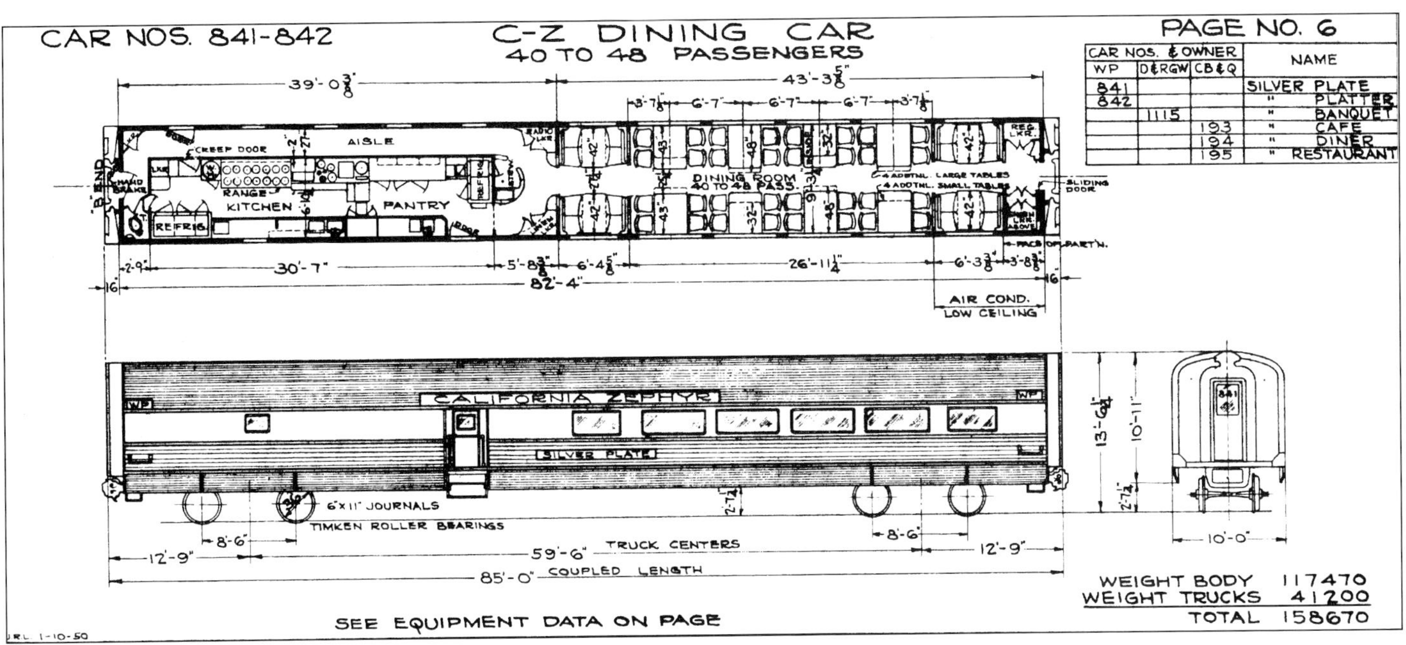

CAR NOS. 841-842
C-Z DINING CAR
40 TO 48 PASSENGERS
PAGE NO. 6
CAR NOS. & OWNER
WP D&RGW CB&Q
NAME
841 SILVER PLATE
842 " PLATTER
1115 " BANQUET
193 " CAFE
194 " DINER
195 " RESTAURANT
AISLE
KITCHEN
PANTRY
RANGE
REFRIG.
DINING ROOM 40 TO 48 PASS.
AIR COND. LOW CEILING
CALIFORNIA ZEPHYR
SILVER PLATE
6"x11" JOURNALS
TIMKEN ROLLER BEARINGS
TRUCK CENTERS
COUPLED LENGTH
WEIGHT BODY 117470
WEIGHT TRUCKS 41200
TOTAL 158670
SEE EQUIPMENT DATA ON PAGE

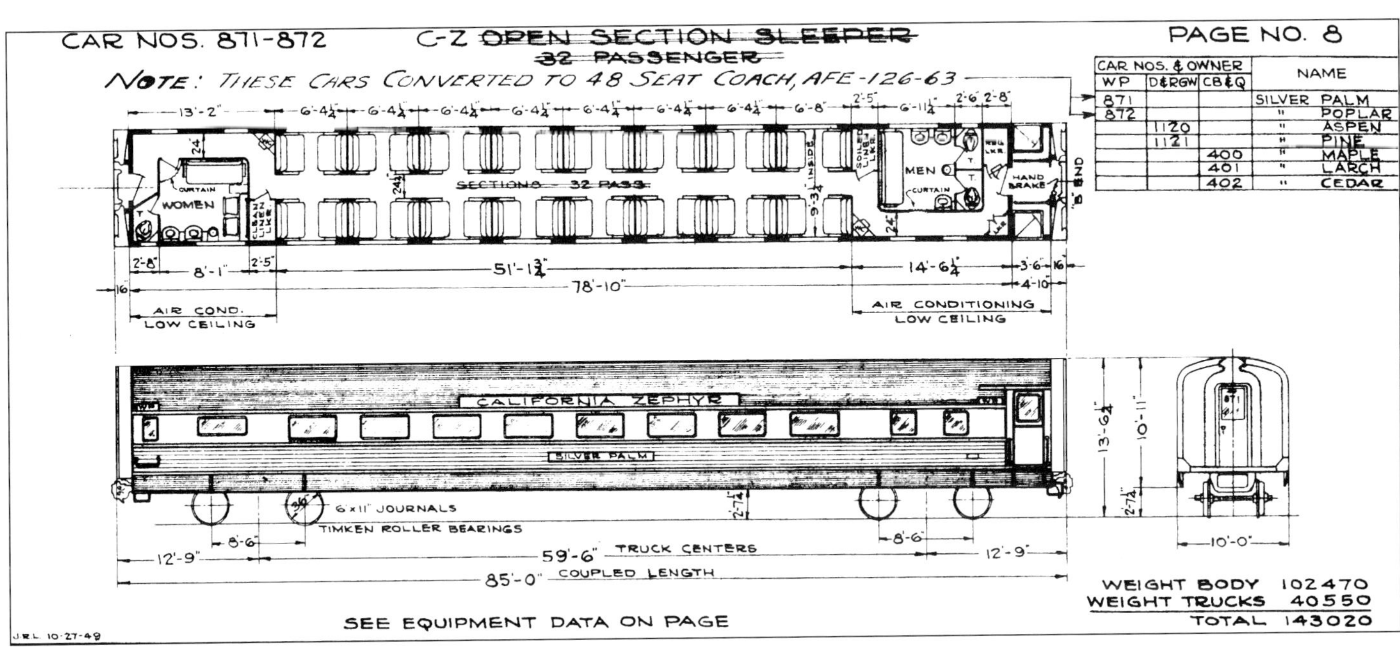

CAR NOS. 871-872
C-Z OPEN SECTION SLEEPER
32 PASSENGER
NOTE: THESE CARS CONVERTED TO 48 SEAT COACH, AFE-126-63
PAGE NO. 8
CAR NOS. & OWNER
WP D&RGW CB&Q
NAME
871 SILVER PALM
872 " POPLAR
1120 " ASPEN
1121 " PINE
400 " MAPLE
401 " LARCH
402 " CEDAR
WOMEN
MEN
SECTIONS 32 PASS
AIR COND. LOW CEILING
AIR CONDITIONING LOW CEILING
CALIFORNIA ZEPHYR
SILVER PALM
6"x11" JOURNALS
TIMKEN ROLLER BEARINGS
TRUCK CENTERS
COUPLED LENGTH
WEIGHT BODY 102470
WEIGHT TRUCKS 40550
TOTAL 143020
SEE EQUIPMENT DATA ON PAGE

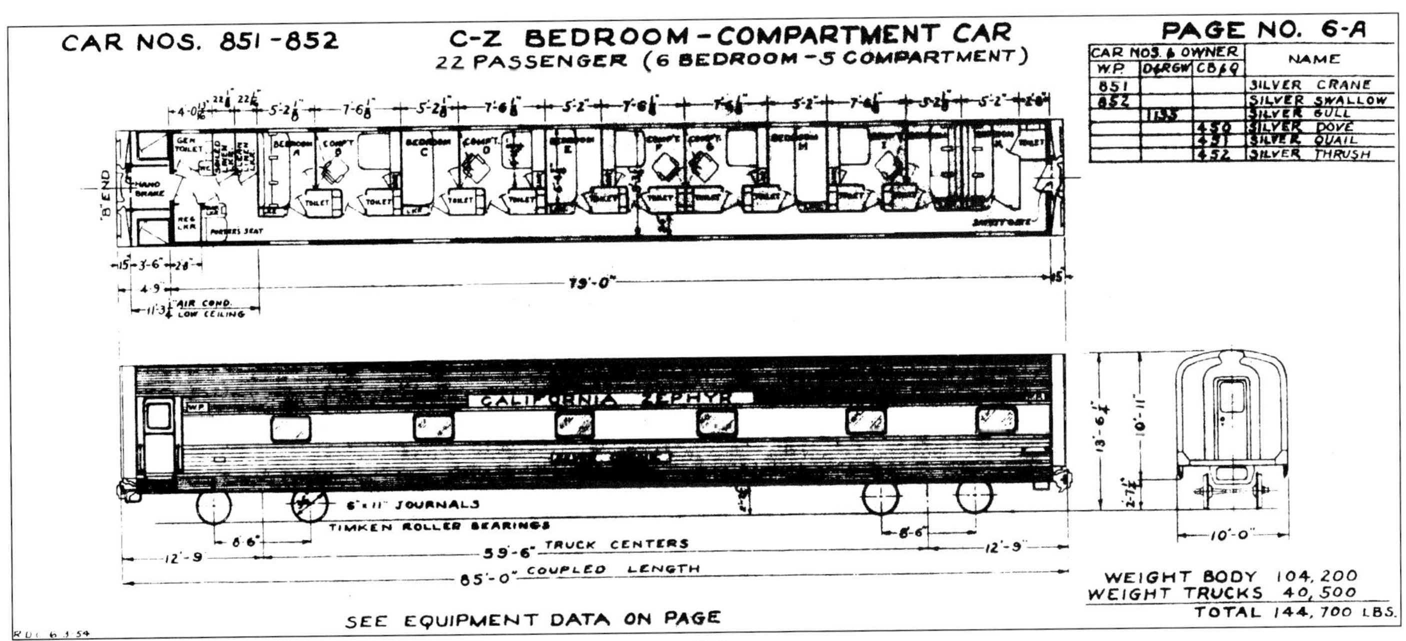

CAR NOS. 851-852
C-Z BEDROOM-COMPARTMENT CAR
22 PASSENGER (6 BEDROOM-5 COMPARTMENT)
PAGE NO. 6-A
CAR NOS. & OWNER
W.P. D&RGW CB&Q
NAME
851 SILVER CRANE
852 SILVER SWALLOW
1135 SILVER GULL
450 SILVER DOVE
451 SILVER QUAIL
452 SILVER THRUSH
AIR COND. LOW CEILING
CALIFORNIA ZEPHYR
6"x11" JOURNALS
TIMKEN ROLLER BEARINGS
TRUCK CENTERS
COUPLED LENGTH
WEIGHT BODY 104,200
WEIGHT TRUCKS 40,500
TOTAL 144,700 LBS.
SEE EQUIPMENT DATA ON PAGE

(above) Precious few passenger trains operated with a dome observation car. This car literally made a superb train even better. WP's *Silver Planet* is shown here on the tail end of train 18 on the CB&Q at Galesburg, Illinois, on December 6, 1964.

(Collection of Louis A. Marre)

(facing page, top) Western Pacific's other dome observation was the *Silver Crescent*, shown here during its air brake test prior to movement from Middle Harbor Yard (Oakland) on March 12, 1966. Note the air gauge instruments below the classic neon *California Zephyr* drumhead.

(Author's Collection)

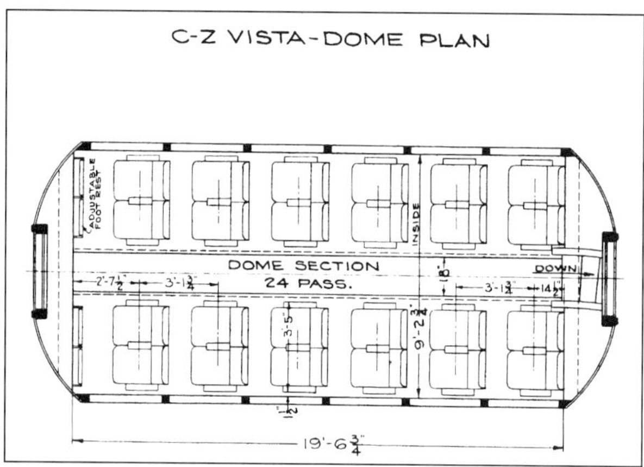

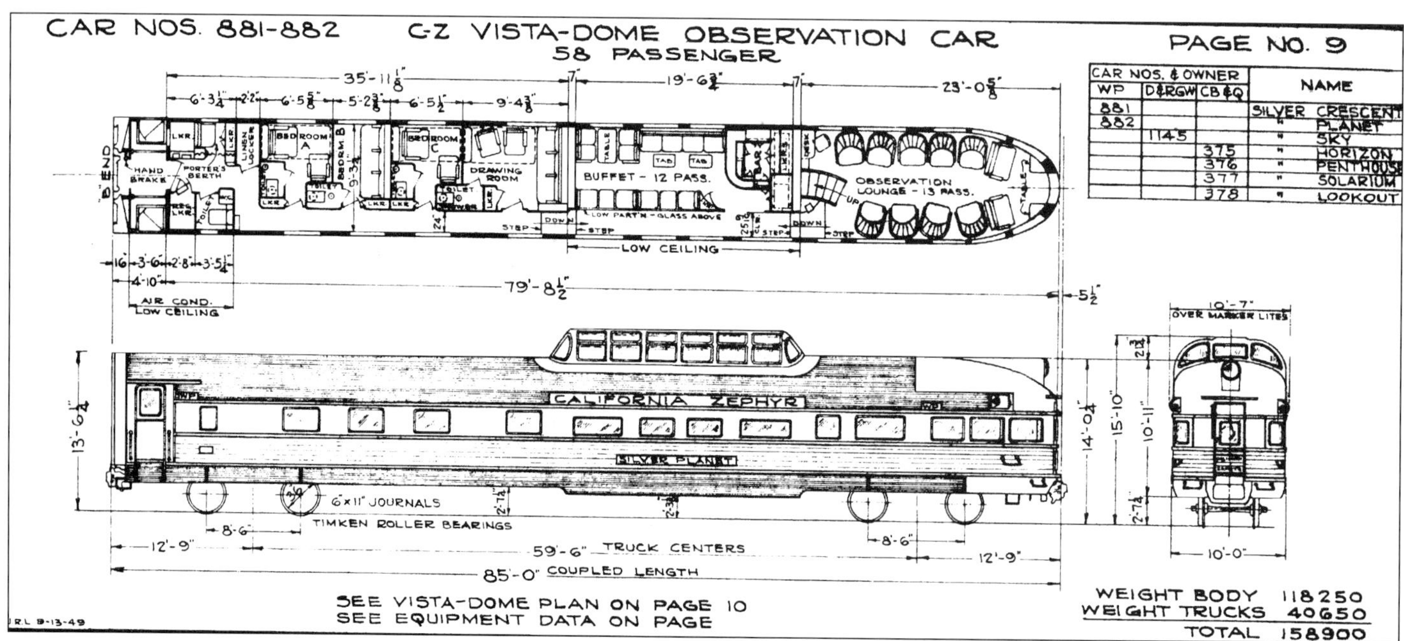

CAR NOS. & OWNER			NAME
WP	D&RGW	CB&Q	
881			SILVER CRESCENT
882			" PLANET
	1145		" SKY
		375	" HORIZON
		376	" PENTHOUSE
		377	" SOLARIUM
		378	" LOOKOUT

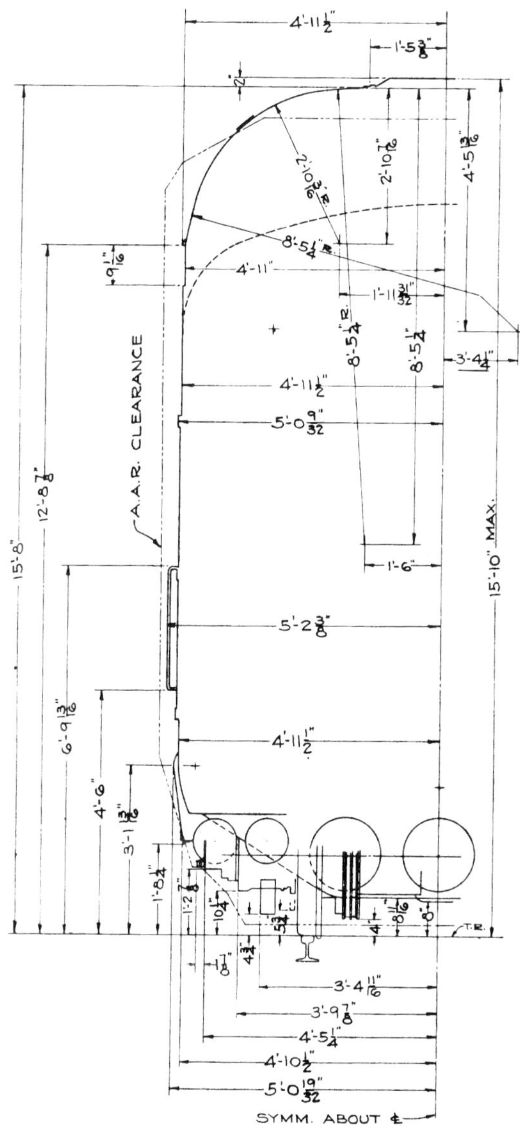

COMPOSITE CLEARANCE DIAGRAM
OF ALL CALIFORNIA ZEPHYR CARS
LIGHT - READY TO RUN

(above) The composite clearance diagram provides an astonishing amount of information about the *CZ's* Budd equipment.

(Author's Collection)

(left) The *California Zephyr* at Oakland in 1958 – one dozen matched cars, including five domes, behind FP7A 804-A and two F3Bs.

(Jim Shaw)

(following page) The *CZ* crosses Rock Creek bridge, westbound in the Feather River Canyon.

(Rail Photo Service)

Western Pacific Lightweight Passenger Equipment

Configuration	Number	Name	Remarks
Baggage	801	Silver Beaver	To Auto-Train 135.
	802	Silver Stag	
Dome Coach	811	Silver Dollar	To Auto-Train 460.
	812	Silver Feather	To Auto-Train 461.
	813	Silver Palace	To Auto-Train 462.
	814	Silver Sage	To Auto-Train 463.
	815	Silver Schooner	To Auto-Train 470.
	816	Silver Scout	To Auto-Train 471.
	817	Silver Thistle	To Auto-Train 464.
Dome Buffet - Dormitory	831	Silver Chalet	
	832	Silver Hostel	
Dining Car	841	Silver Plate	
	842	Silver Platter	
6 Double Bedroom - 5 Cptmt.	851	Silver Crane	
	852	Silver Swallow	
10 Roomette - 6 Dbl. Bedroom	861	Silver Arroyo	
	862	Silver Canyon	To SP Dynamometer Car 252.
	863	Silver Mountain	
	864	Silver Palisade	
	865	Silver Range	
	866	Silver Bay	
	867	Silver Surf	
Sixteen Section Tourist Sleeper	871	Silver Palm	Converted to 48-seat Coach in 1963. To Auto-Train 580.
	872	Silver Poplar	Converted to 48-seat Coach in 1963. To Auto-Train 582.
3 Double Bedroom - Drawing Room - Dome - Observation	881	Silver Crescent	
	882	Silver Planet	

(WP Photo, TLC Collection)

Zephyrette – what a superb name for a Rail Diesel Car, in view of the *California Zephyr's* popularity. Although the two cars were practically off-the-shelf Budd RDC-2s, they did carry numberboards as well as the name *Zephyrette* just behind the baggage door. Car 375 is seen (left) at Oakland in 1959.

(Author's Collection)

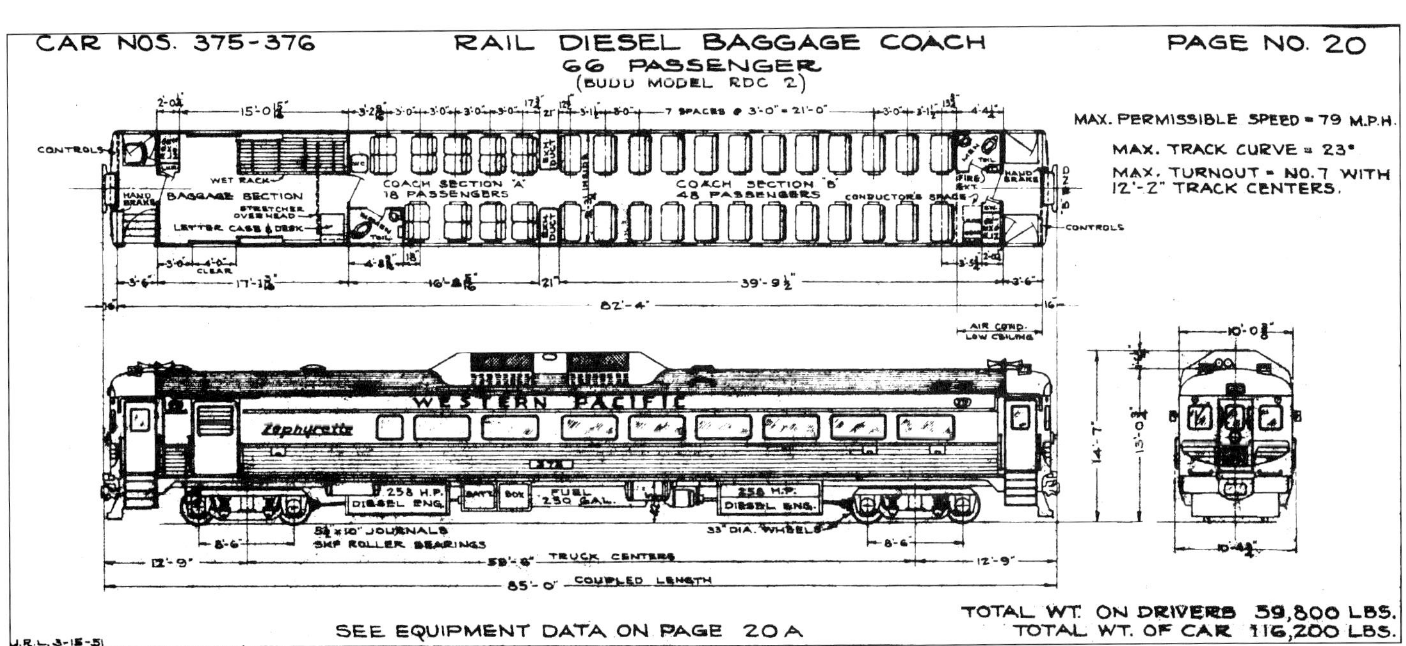

4 Freight Equipment

The focus of this chapter is the freight equipment operated by the Western Pacific. The company owned a wide variety of freight cars for the use of its shippers between Salt Lake City and Oakland. The WP had a strong and positive working relationship between itself and the shipping public, the result of a high level maintenance program as well as precision scheduling of its freight services. This pictorial review includes diagrams, rosters and photographs of WP equipment from the post World War II period.

40-foot car 20750 (series 20551-20800) had a seven-foot door. Built in June 1947 by the Mt.Vernon Car Manufacturing Division of the Pressed Steel Car Company. Painted box car red with white lettering. *(John Ryczkowski Collection)*

Box Cars

(facing page, top) In 1952 Pullman-Standard built two 40-foot cushion underframe PS-1 test cars for WP. Numbered 1952 and 1953, they had a spectacular orange and black paint scheme.
(John Ryczkowski)

(above) WP box cars were painted and lettered in a variety of schemes. 40-foot PS-1 21279 (series 20821-21400) has "WESTERN PACIFIC" boldly spelled out. "Feather River Route" graces the area normally reserved for a WP insignia. Painted box car red with white lettering, with a seven foot Youngstown door.
(John Ryczkowski)

(left) The 40-foot box car with a six-foot door was a standard on most railroads. WP 20279, painted box car red with white lettering, was part of series 20201-20550. Oakland, California, August 10, 1961.
(Collection of Howard W. Ameling)

(left) An ultra plain WP lettering scheme on 40-foot car 22014 (series 22001-22025). Equipped with a seven-foot door, the interior had plyveneer sides and ends coated with Imron for flour loading.
(John Ryczkowski)

(below) Moving on to the 50-foot cars, orange and black PS-1 3030 (3011-3050, later 3331-3373) had an Evans DF loader and a cushion underframe.
(John Ryczkowski)

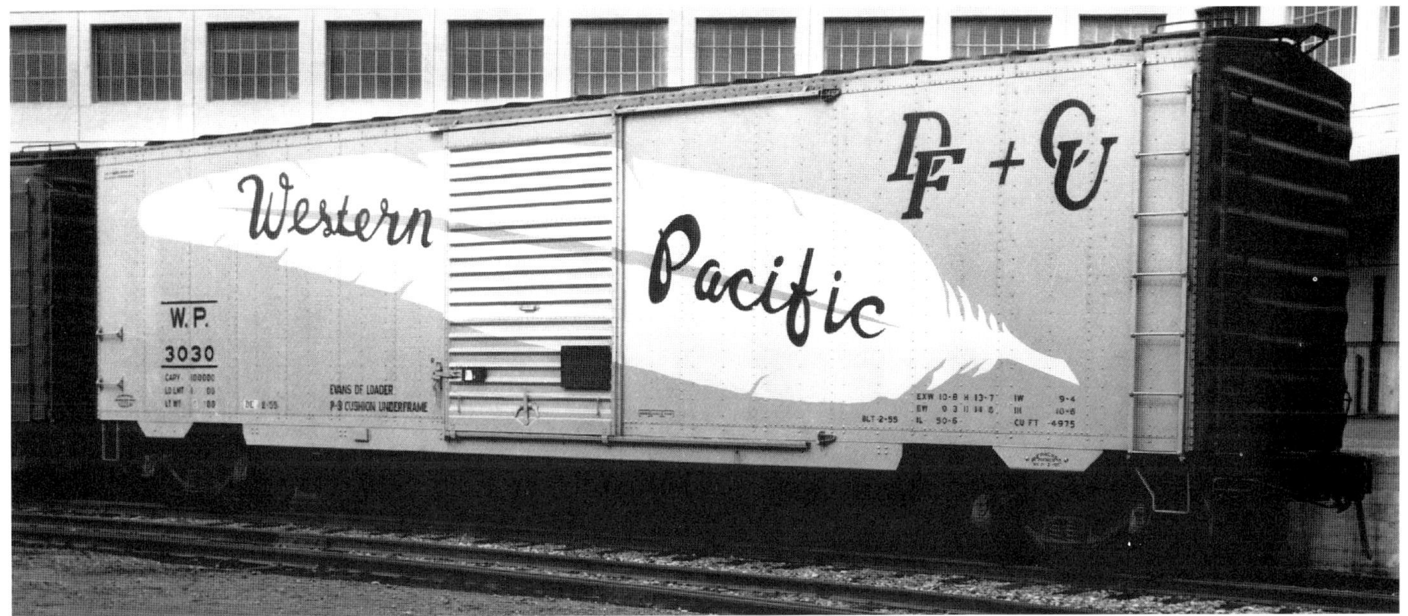

(left) 50-foot PS-1 3373 in a box car red scheme with a different company slogan – "The Western Way," which is just about faded out under the large "WP." Photographed at Winnemucca, Nevada, in December 1982.

(Bob Larson)

(left) Plug door box car 60301 (60301-60340) was 50 feet, 1 inch long inside and could handle 147,000 pounds. It was equipped with a special cushioning device, crossmember type loaders, and was not intended for bulk loading. The car is seen in service at Winnemucca, Nevada, in December 1983.

(Bob Larson)

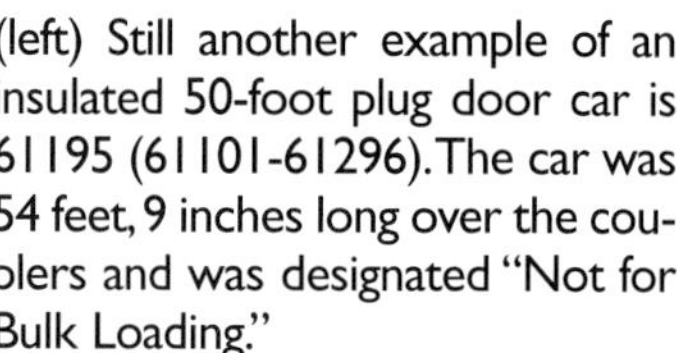

(left) Still another example of an insulated 50-foot plug door car is 61195 (61101-61296). The car was 54 feet, 9 inches long over the couplers and was designated "Not for Bulk Loading."

(John Ryczkowski)

(below) 67009 (67007-67019) was a special 60-foot plug door insulated car with load dividers, adjustable side wall fillers, and the designation "Not for bulk loading."

(Collection of the Author)

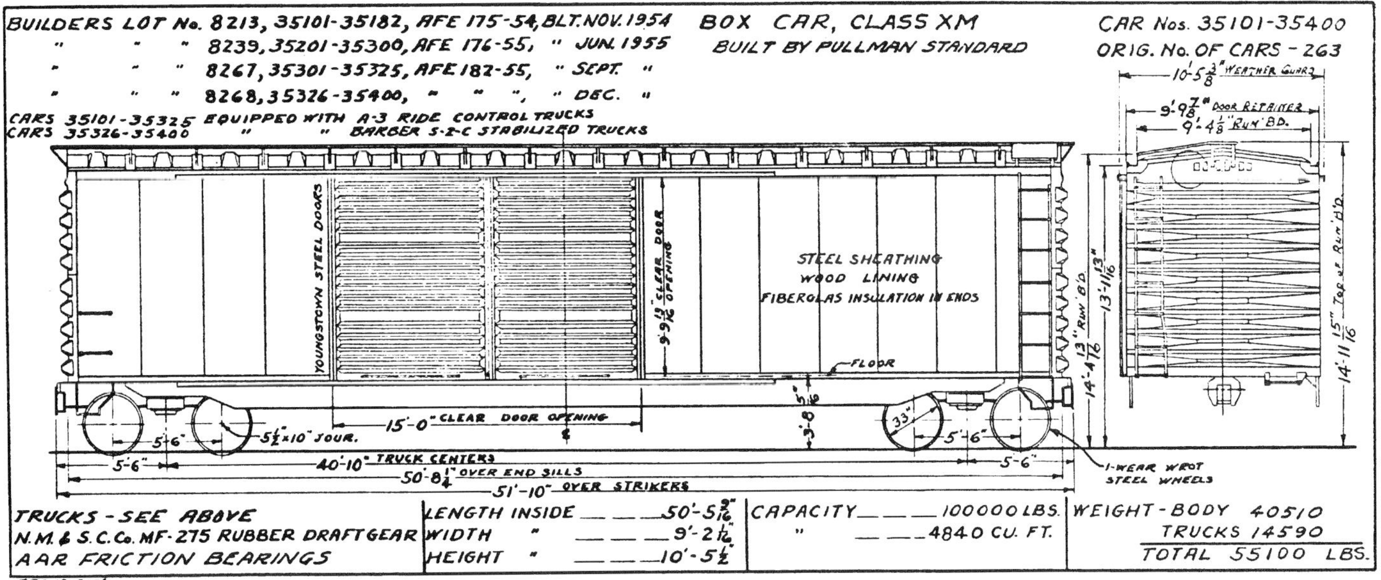

(top) What about the 50-foot double door box cars? Side view shows car 35263 (35101-35400), equipped with a 15-foot door opening. By the time this car was photographed, its roof walk had been removed.

(John Ryczkowski)

(right) PS-1 34005 (34004-34023) had 55-ton trucks and P-S doors; was painted with the slogan, "The Western Way." Seen at Portola in August 1984.

(Bob Larson)

(right) Later developments in the 50-foot car came in the form of outside post designs like WP 38298 (38226-38325), built by Pacific Car and Foundry in early 1980. They were the only cars delivered new with this stylized herald. Photographed in the consist of BN's Stillwater (Minnesota) local at White Bear Lake, Minnesota, in June 1980.

(Thomas A. Dorin)

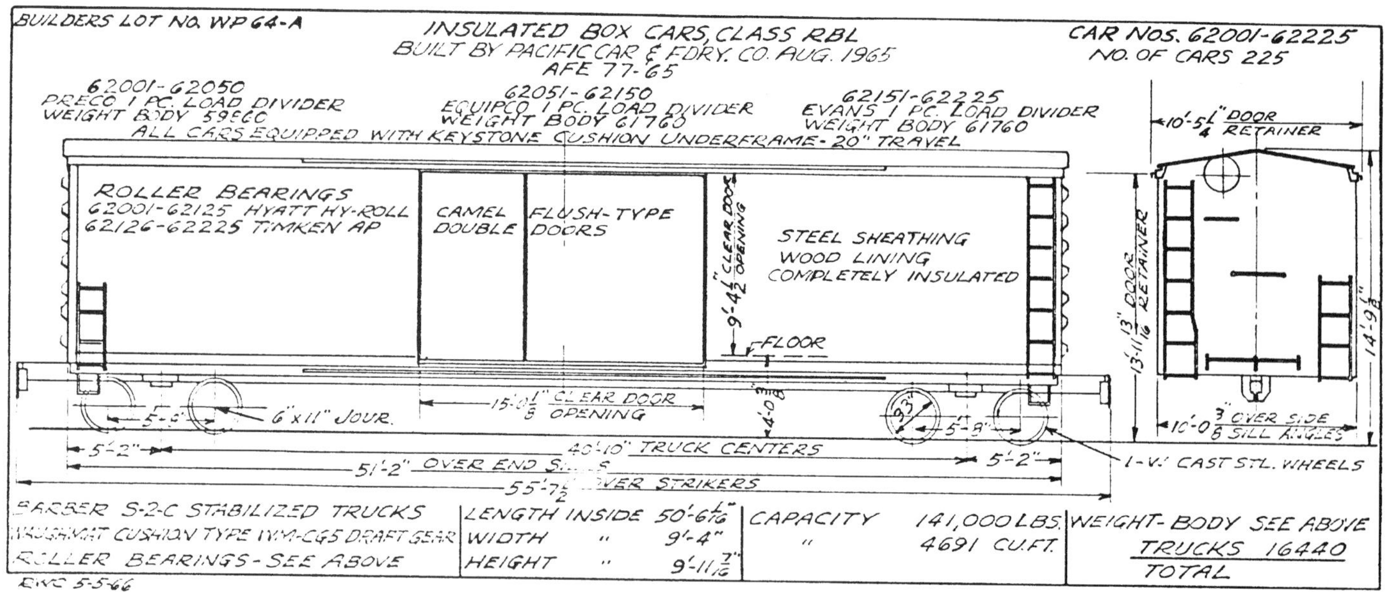

The next development in WP box cars was the 50-foot double plug door design. WP 62182 (62051-62225) is an insulated car with a special cushion device and load dividers, designated "Not for Bulk Loading." Seen in service at Yuba City, California, in March 1984.

(Bob Larson)

50-foot double plug door car 64064 (64001-64075) is very similar to the 62182. It has been repainted, retaining box car red but with the modern feather insignia.

(John Ryckowski)

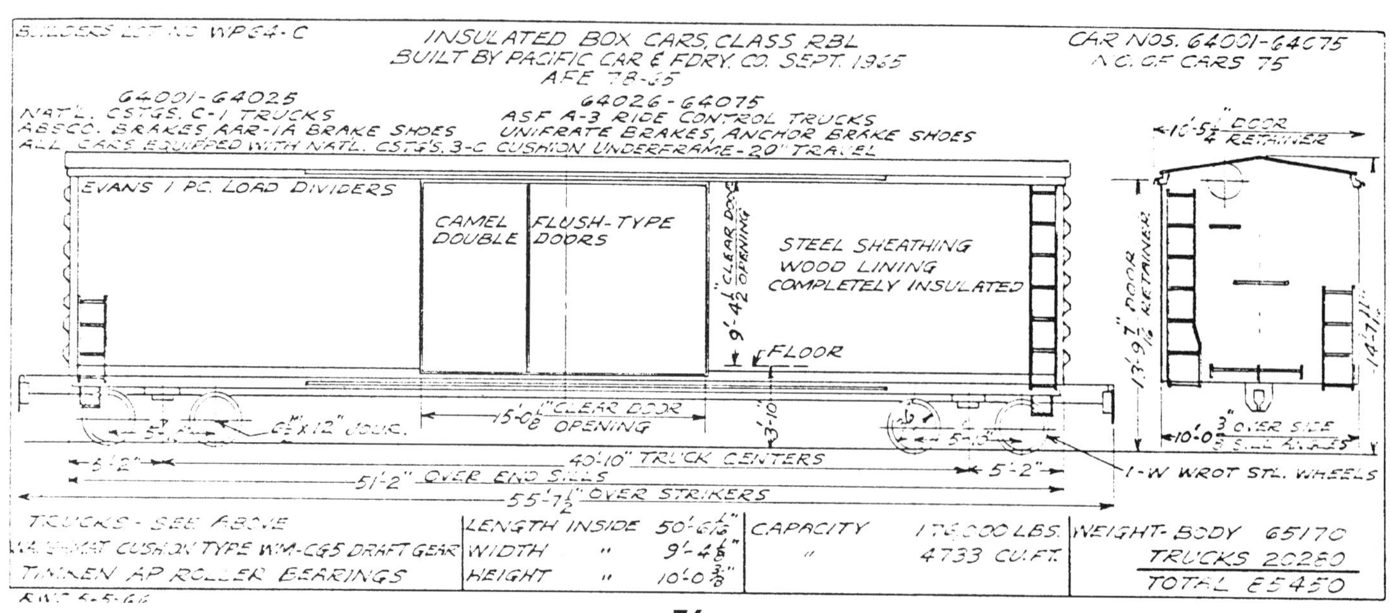

Western Pacific 64708 (64701-64748) is still another type of 50-foot insulated car, with a double-width plug door. Capacity was 138,000 pounds, with a special cushion device, Dual Air Pak load dividers, and the designation "Not for Bulk Loading." Seen on the Grand Trunk Western in Lansing, Michigan, during the summer of 1985.

(Michael A. Dorin)

WP 64956 (64951-64995) is fully insulated and also equipped with an extra-wide plug door. Council Bluffs, Iowa, July 29, 1989.

(George R. Cockle, Collection of Howard Ameling)

WP 65274 (65201-65400) is an insulated car built in 1974 for can goods service with a 52 foot, 6 inch inside length (60 feet, 6 inches over couplers), equipped with Dual Air Pak load dividers. Capacity was listed in pounds (137,000) and kilograms (62150).

(John Ryczkowski)

(below) 69-foot 3714 is part of series 3701-3725. Council Bluffs, Iowa, June 16, 1988.

(George R. Cockle, Collection of Howard Ameling)

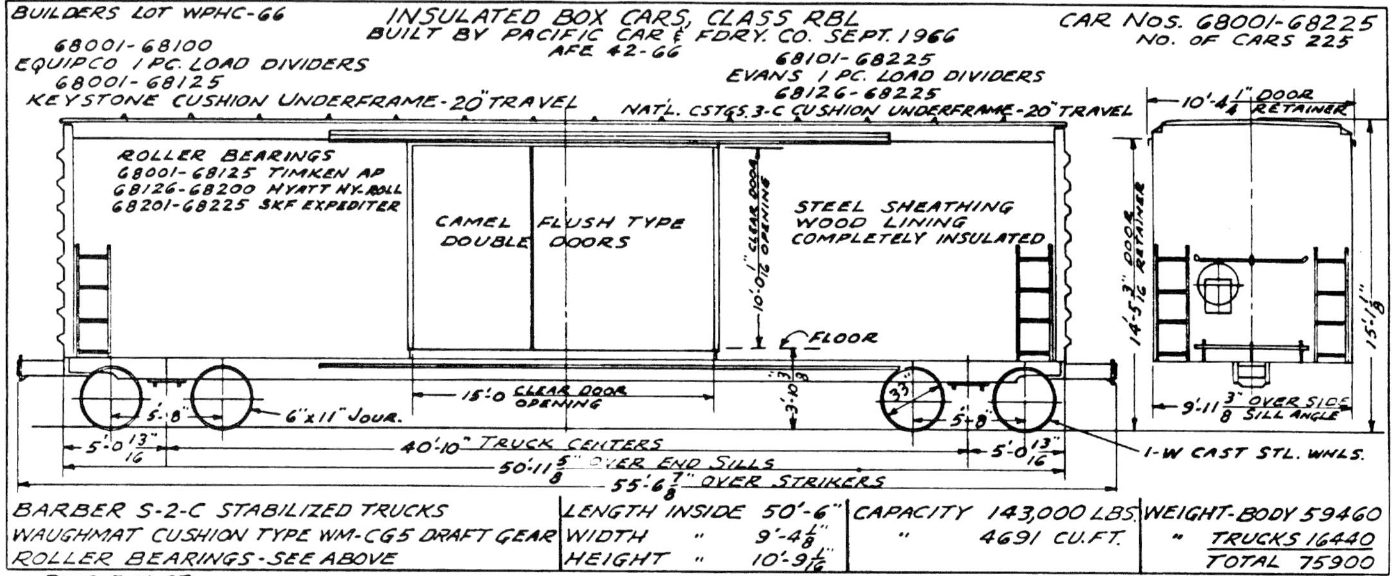

(top) WP 68169 is one of several cars in series 68001-68225 that were repainted orange with the classic WP insignia that had not been used for several years. This car was repainted at Sacramento in March, 1979.

(John Ryczkowski)

(right) WP 3152 (3151-3167) is a 67-foot car equipped with a 10-foot sliding door. Council Bluffs, Iowa, August 14, 1989.

(George R. Cockle, Collection of Howard Ameling)

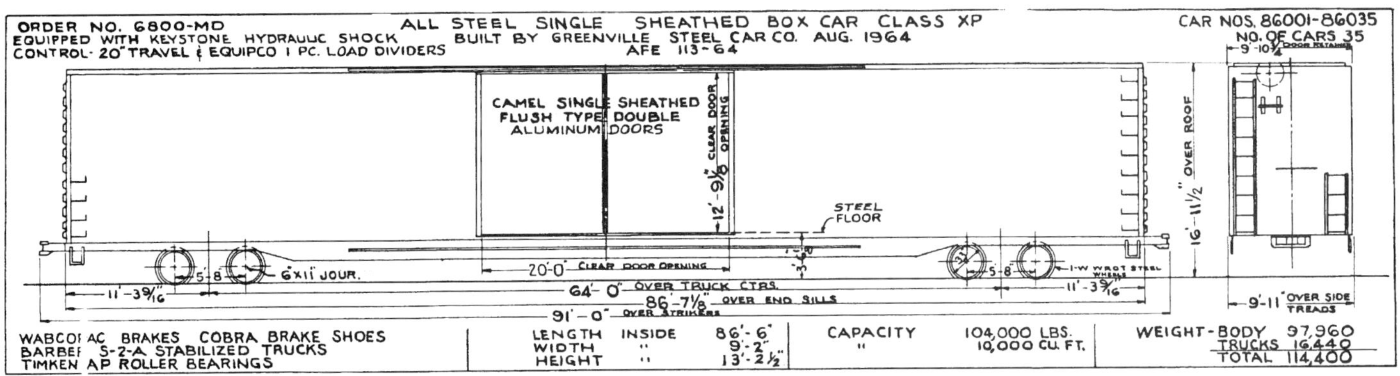

(above) 91 feet over strikers – now that is a big box car. WP 86005 is an auto parts car built in 1964. The capacity of series 86001-86035 is 104,000 pounds.

(Author's Collection)

(below) Double plug door auto parts car 86067 is similar, but with a slightly different lettering scheme. Series 86042-86077. Seen at Portola, California, in July 1980.

(Bob Larson)

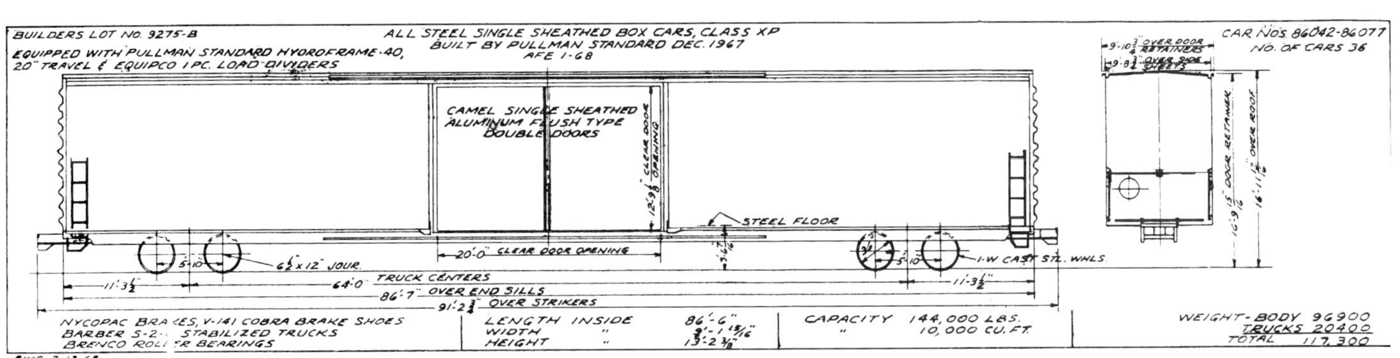

Refrigerator Cars

Pacific Fruit Express is known mostly for its Union Pacific and Southern Pacific refrigerator cars, but indeed, Western Pacific was also part of the picture. Wood reefers, such as 52405 built in 1924, carried PFE reporting marks and WP insignias. For a photo of this series in work service, see Chapter 5.
(John Ryczkowski)

Modern refrigerator car service on Western Pacific was provided by cars leased from Fruit Growers Express with WPRX reporting marks, such as 97002 shown here.
(John Ryczkowski)

Hopper Cars

WP was never a large owner of hopper cars, but what they did have were 100-ton capacity. WP 10128 (series 10086-10200) was rated at 203,000 pounds. Inside length was 39 feet (44 feet, 5 inches over couplers). Seen in taconite pellet service between the Mesabi Iron Range (Minnesota) and Provo, Utah, via the Duluth, Missabe & Iron Range Railway, C&NW and UP. Council Bluffs, Iowa, March 21, 1989.
(George R. Cockle, Collection of Howard Ameling)

(top) Triple hopper 10116 only carried WP reporting marks. WP hoppers were painted black with white lettering. Seen at Superior, Wisconsin, in March 1989.

(This page, Author's Collection unless noted)

(middle) Car 10221 (series 10201-10230) was part of a smaller group of cars with only two hopper bays. Superior, Wisconsin, March 1989.

(above) Twin hopper 10502 is part of series 10301-10575. Council Bluffs, Iowa, September 9, 1989.

(George R. Cockle, Collecton of Howard Ameling)

(below) WP triple hopper 10290 (10231-10295). Superior, Wisconsin, March 1989.

(middle) Side discharge gates mark 10790 (series 10701-10800) as a ballast car.

(John Ryczkowski)

(bottom) WP 10904 (10801-11000) in stone service on MP. Note the differences in ladders and grab irons.

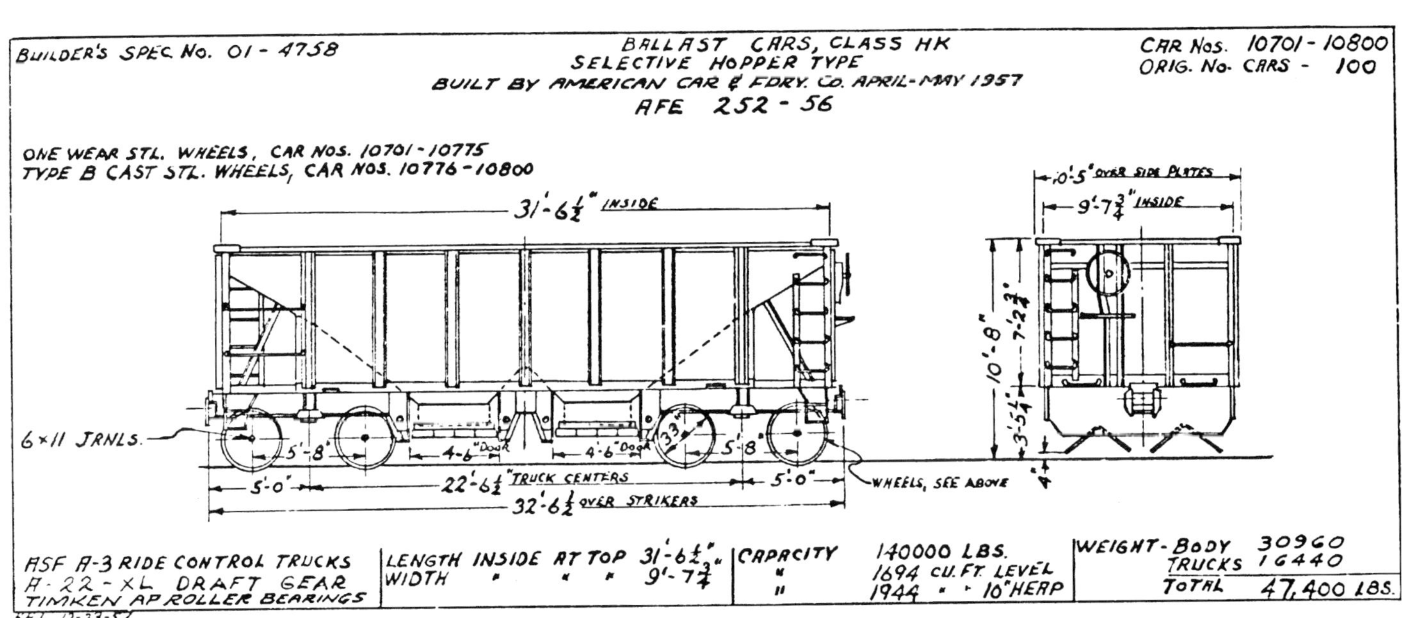

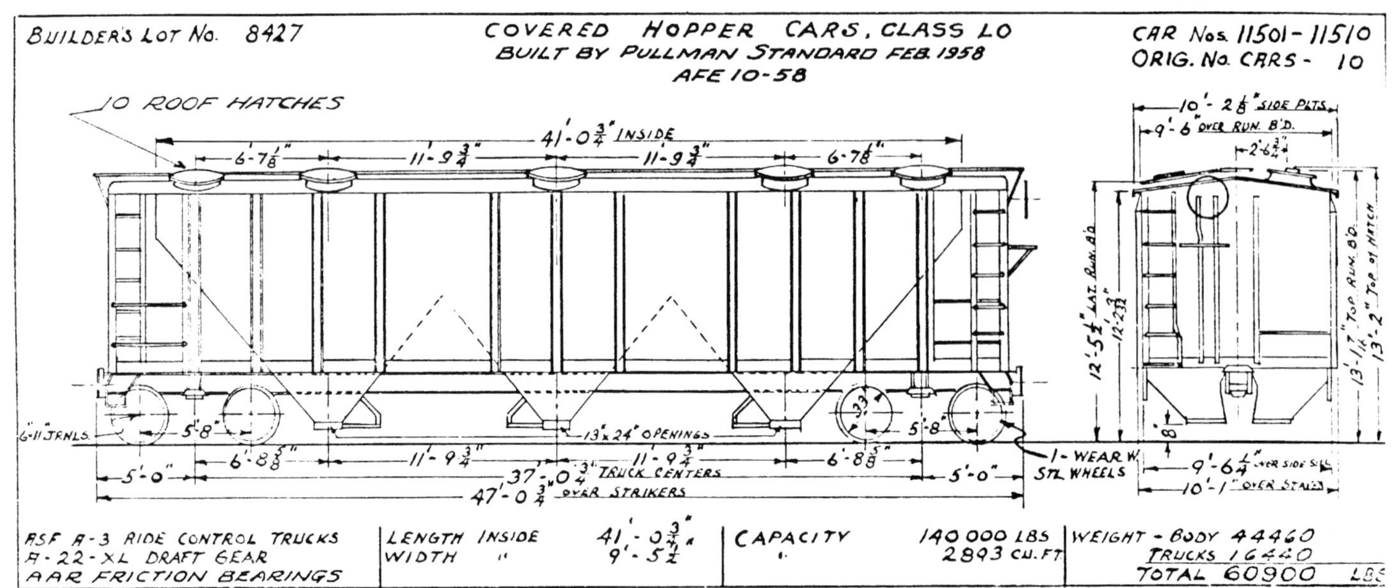

WP covered hopper 11509 (11501-11510) was part of a small group of Pullman-Standard PS-2s. These triple hoppers had a capacity of 2,893 cubic feet. The "WESTERN PACIFIC" lettering is barely visible in the upper right corner.
(John Ryczkowski)

Single bay Airslide™ covered hopper 11624 (series 11617-11662) was equipped with six roof hatches, had a 2,600 cubic foot capacity.
(John Ryczkowski)

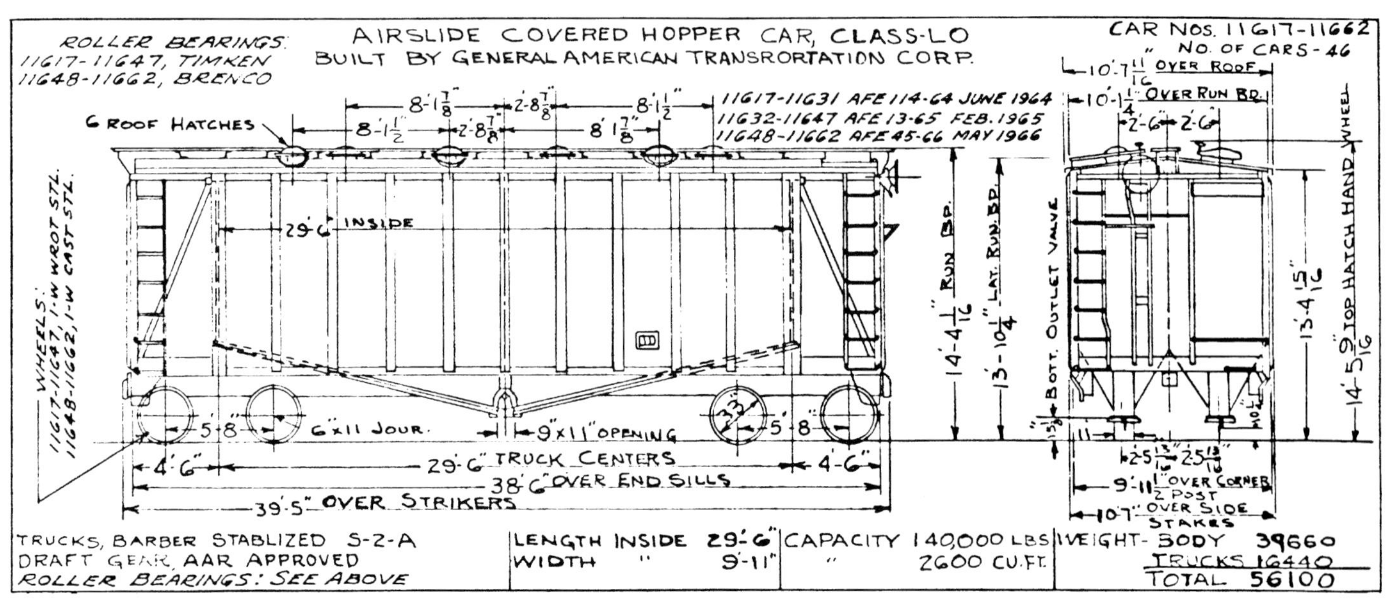

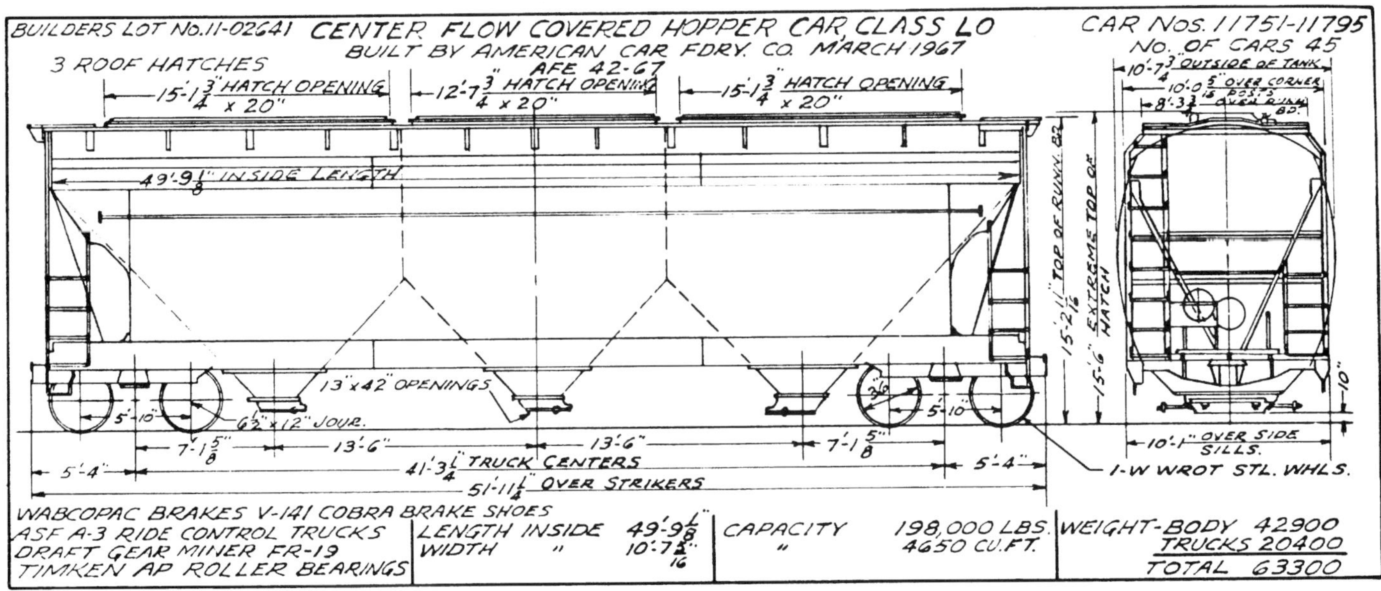

Western Pacific operated an extensive and varied fleet of 100 ton capacity jumbo covered hoppers. Car 11773 (11751-11800) is an ACF Center Flow™ car with a 4,650 cubic foot capacity.
(John Ryczkowski)

Covered hopper 11881 (11851-11900) was built by Magor Car in 1967. Made of aluminum, the car's capacity was listed as 4,750 cubic feet, with a load limit of 208,500 pounds.
(John Ryczkowski)

ALUMINUM CENTER FLOW COVERED HOPPER, CLASS LO — CAR NOS. 11851-11900
BUILT BY MAGOR CAR CORP. 11851-11875, AFE 12-65 JULY 1965; 11876-11900, AFE 44-66 APRIL 1967 — NO OF CARS 50
3 ROOF HATCHES
16'-4 7/8" HATCH OPENING x 20 3/4" — 13'-11 3/4" OPENING x 20 3/4" — 16'-4 7/8" OPENING x 20 3/4"
℄ CAR
14'-6 25/32" TOP RUNN. BD. — 14'-11 11/32" EXTREME TOP OF HATCH
10'-5 15/16" SIDE POST — 9'-11 1/2" CORNER POST
6 1/2" x 12" JOUR. — 5'-10 — 8'-1 1/2" — 14'-5 1/2" — 45'-2" TRUCK CENTERS — 4'-11 1/2" — 55'-1" OVER STRIKERS
24" x 30" OPENINGS, CARS 11851-11875; 31 5/8" x 34" OPENINGS, CARS 11876-11900
11 3/16" CARS 11851-11875; 9 7/8" CARS 11876-11900
1-W WROT STL. WHLS.

WABCOPAC BRAKES V-141 COBRA BRAKE SHOES TRUCKS, BARBER STABILIZED S-2-A DRAFT GEAR, AAR APPROVED TIMKEN AP ROLLER BEARINGS	LENGTH INSIDE 54'-1" WIDTH " 9'-10"	CAPACITY 207,000 LBS " 4750 CU.FT.	WEIGHT BODY 34200 TRUCKS 20,400 TOTAL 54,600

JCS 7-2-68

(above) ACF Center Flow™ 11927 (11901-11965) was built in 1974. Outside length of the car was 54 feet, 6 inches with a capacity of 197,000 pounds.

(John Ryczkowski)

(left) Still another WP ACF Center Flow™ car was the 11983 (11966-12000). It was slightly longer than the 11901 series at 57 feet, 11 inches. Capacity was 198,000 pounds.

(John Ryczkowski)

(left) Series 12001-12050 is represented by WP 12023, with an outside length of 54 feet, 6 inches and a capacity of 196,000 pounds. Seen at St. Paul, Minnesota, in 1986.

(Author's Collection)

Covered hopper 12066 was built in 1980 with a 57 foot, 9 inch outside length and a capacity of 197,000 pounds. Part of series 12051-12100, these cars were among the last purchased by the WP. Photographed in service at Winnemucca, Nevada, in February 1984.

(Bob Larson)

Western Pacific single bay Airslide™ cars NAHX 60300-60309 were built by General American Transportation Corporation in August 1963 and were leased from North American Car Corporation. 60302 was photographed in St. Paul, Minnesota.

(Bob Blomquist)

Flat Cars

(above) Flat car 13215 was renumbered from the 2401-2700 series. It has a 50-foot long floor and a capacity of 55 tons.
(John Ryczkowski)

(right) What appears to be an ordinary 70-ton flat is actually half of a two unit model joined by locked couplers. WP 898-A and its traveling companion were renumbered from the 2401-2700 series to carry 20-foot containers.
(John Ryczkowski)

(right) Sixty foot flat 2171 (2161-2175) was built in 1967, and has been pressed into service by the demise of UP 39490.
(John Ryczkowski)

It is natural that the Western Pacific would have Center Beam flat cars on its roster. The company served extensive forest areas, and WP 1405 (series 1401-1410) was rated at 168,000 pounds capacity, measured 60 feet, 8 inches inside length and 68 feet long over the couplers.
(John Ryczkowski)

Bilevel auto rack for handling pick-up trucks, vans and other highway vehicles. Riding on yellow Trailer Train flats, the WP racks were painted box car red with bare metal screens and white lettering.
(Author's Collection)

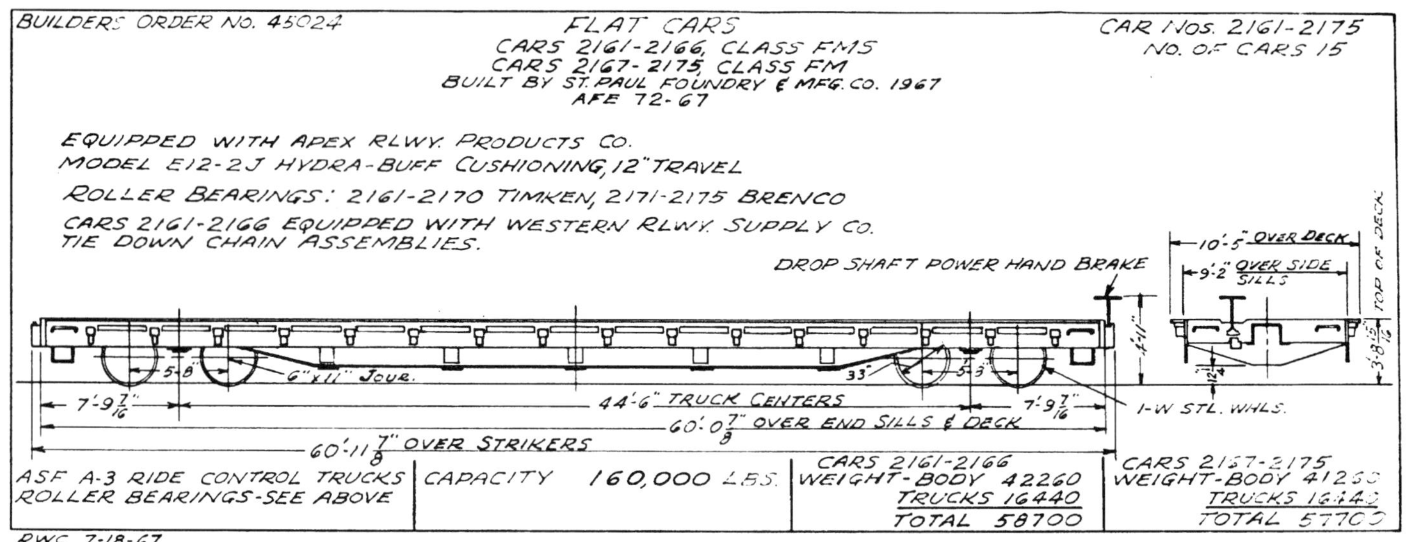

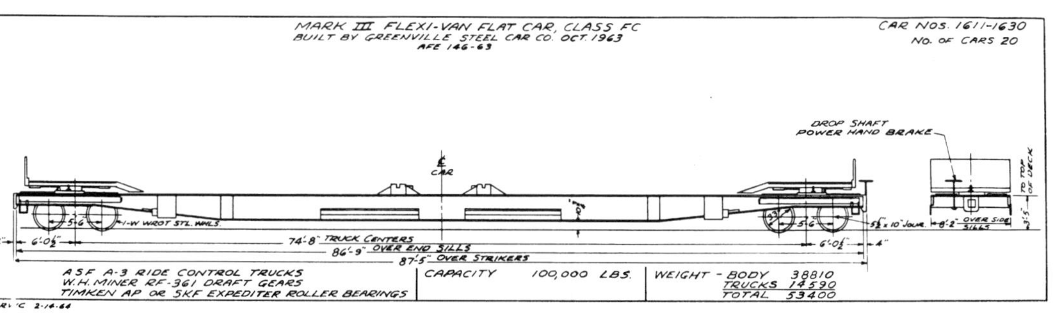

A little known fact is that WP operated Mark III Flexi-van cars, series 1611-1630, shown in the diagram at left.
(Western Pacific Railroad, Collection of the Author)

Gondolas

WP 6053 (6051-6060) is a 52 foot, 6 inch covered gon and carries an orange WP feather with yellow lettering.
(John Ryczkowski)

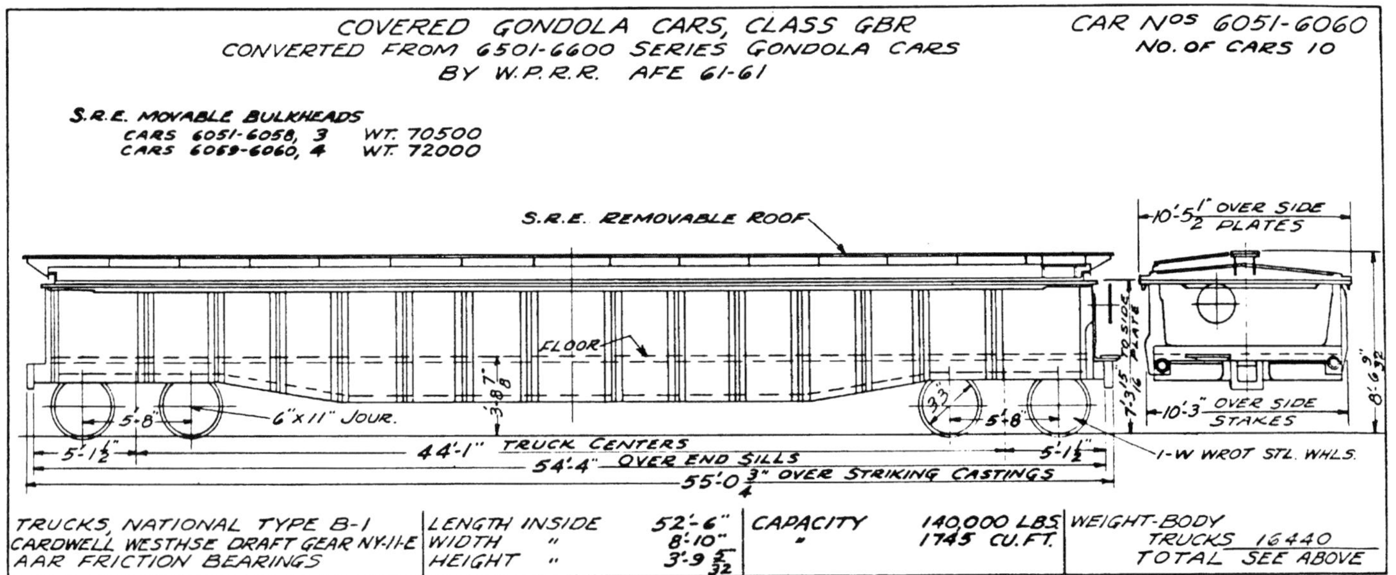

BUILDERS SPECIF. № 10081

DROP END GONDOLA CAR A.A.R. DESIGN, CL.GB CAR NOS. 6501-6600
BUILT BY MT. VERNON CAR MFG. CO. 1945. (OCT.) ORIG. NO. OF CARS 100
AFE 150-44

NOTE: STOCKTON CAR DUMPER CANNOT HANDLE THESE CARS.

52'-6" INSIDE. 44'-1" TRUCK CENTERS. 54'-4" OVER END SILLS. 55'-0 3/4" OVER STRIKING CASTINGS. 6"x11" JOUR. 1 W. WROT. STL. WHLS. 10'-3 1/8" OVER SIDE ANGLES. 9'-6" INSIDE. 10'-3" OVER SIDE STAKES.

TRUCKS NATIONAL TYPE B-1, 70 TON C.S. FRAME WITH INTEGRAL BOX CARDWELL WESTHSE, DRAFT GEAR NY-11-E AAR FRICTION BEARINGS	LENGTH INSIDE 52'-6" WIDTH " 9'-6" HEIGHT " 3'-6 3/8"	CAPACITY 140000 LBS. " 1745 CU.FT. LEVEL FULL	WEIGHT - BODY 42260 " TRUCKS 16440 " TOTAL - 58700 LBS.

(above) WP 6516 (6501-6600) was equipped with drop ends and a wood floor.
(John Ryczkowski)

(above) WP had a fleet of heavy duty 34 foot, 6 inch gondolas equipped with steel cradles for coiled strip steel service. 6406 (6401-6500) is shown at Winnemucca, Nevada.
(John Ryczkowski)

(right) WP 4407 (4401-4425) at Salt Lake City in 1981.
(Thomas A. Dorin)

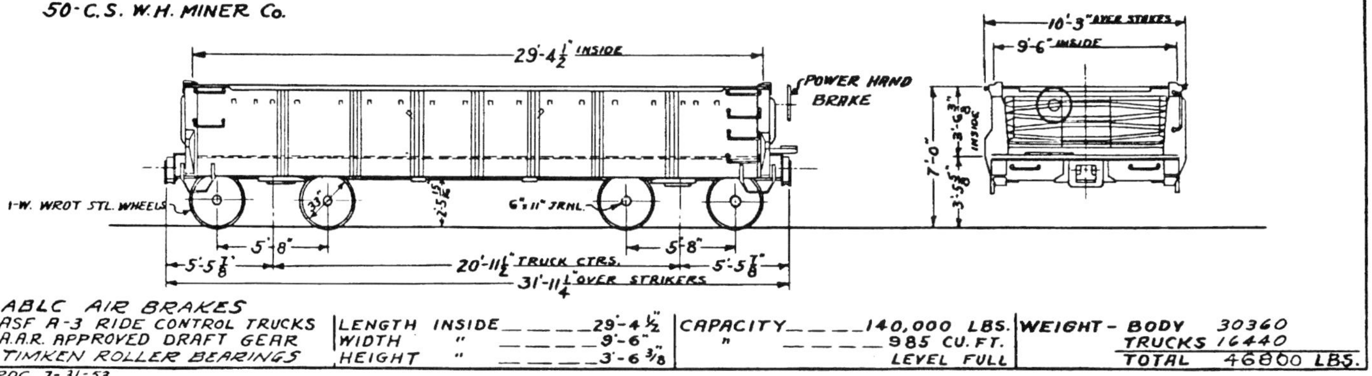

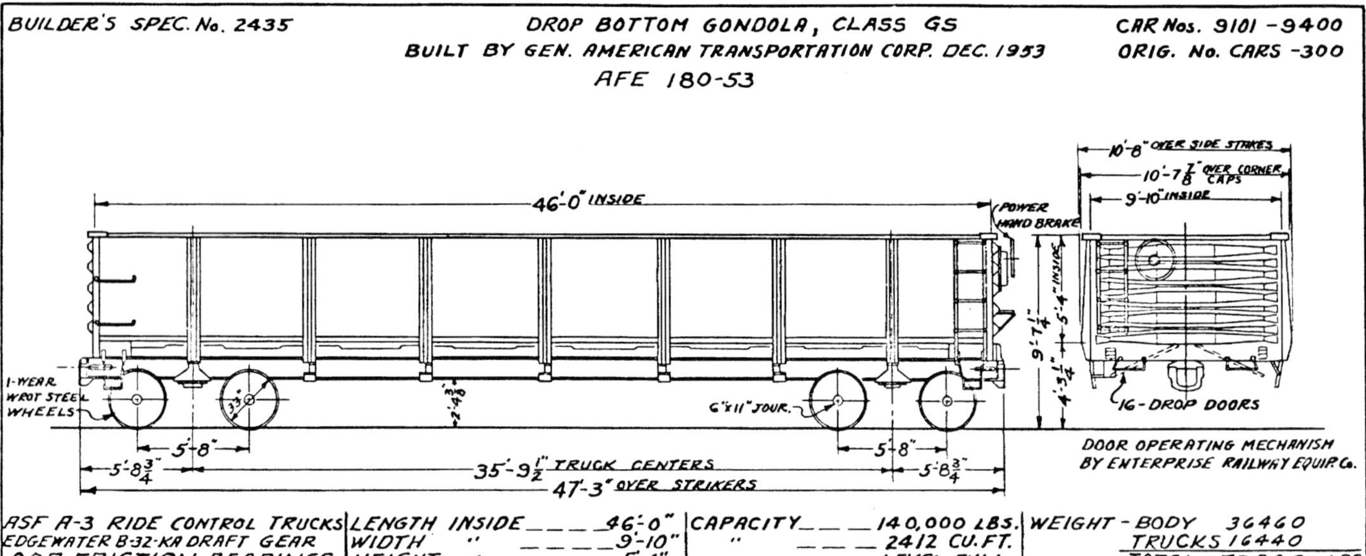

Drop bottom gondola 5001 (renumbered from series 9101-9400). The car's lettering was all but lost when photographed in service at Salt Lake City in August 1988.

(Thomas A. Dorin)

Western Pacific drop bottom gon 5002 was equipped with high sides for wood chip service. The car was lettered "Keep California Green."

(John Ryczkowski)

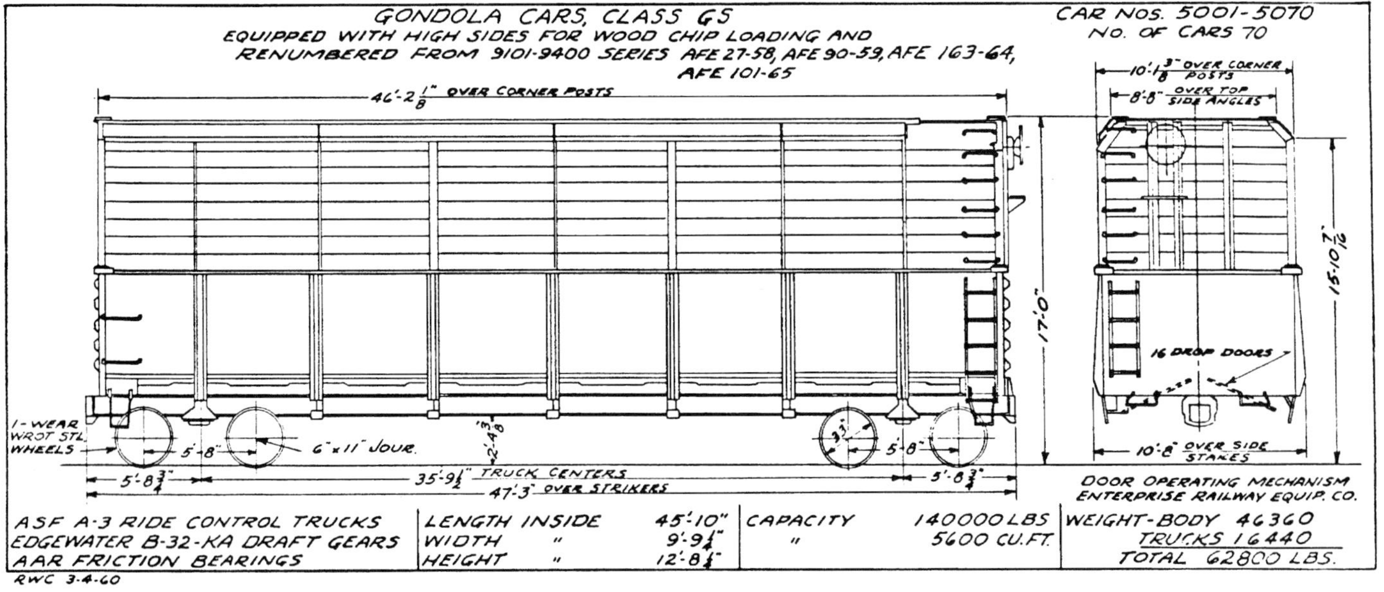

The Western Pacific also operated a fleet of wood chip cars that were built in 1972 by Maxon. Car 5107 (5101-5112) had an outside length of 64 feet, 8 inches and a 192,000 pound capacity.

(John Ryczkowski)

WP's small fleet of shorty gondolas virtually fell into the ore car category. The cars, such as 6208 (6201-6210), could handle 106 tons of payload. They were acquired after the Oro Dam was constructed. This photo of 6208, taken in service at Elko, Nevada, on August 13, 1983, illustrates the final WP scheme on these cars.

(Bob Larson)

This earlier photo of WP 6208 illustrates the lettering scheme after purchase from the Oro Dam contractors.

(John Ryczkowski)

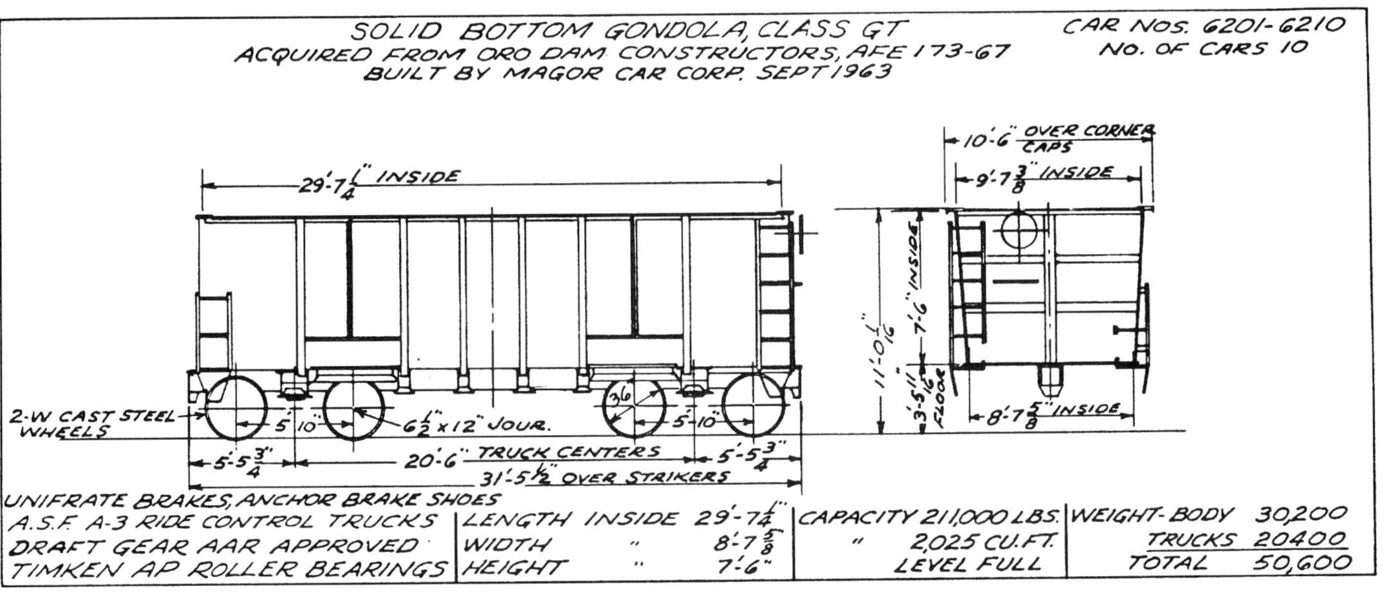

Highway Trailers

(above) Western Pacific 40-foot piggyback trailers painted for the 1976 Bicentennial celebration. Seen in service at Oroville, California, on March 30, 1976.
(Bob Larson)

(left) Western Pacific trailer with the stylized feather insignia. Note the subsidiary WPX Freight Systems, Inc., trailer to the left.
(John Ryczkowski)

Western Pacific Freight Equipment of the 1950s

BOX CARS

Series	Door Opening	Remarks
40-foot single door, 40-ton capacity		
16001-18500	6-0	Steel underframe
26001-26125		
27001-27600		
40-foot single door, 50-ton capacity		
1952-1953	6-0	PS-1
1961-1970	8-0	
3401-3410	8-0	
14301-14540	6-0	
19001-19050	6-0	
19501-19542	7-0	
20001-20200	6-0	
20201-20550	6-0	
20551-20800	7-0	
20821-21400	7-0	PS-1
40-foot double door, 50-ton capacity		
18501-18505	12-0	
50-foot single door, 50-ton capacity		
3001-3010	7-6	
3011-3050	8-0	PS-1
36001-36025	8-0	
55901-55920	7-7 plug	Insulated

BOX CARS (cont'd)

Series	Door Opening	Remarks
55926-55950	8-7 plug	Insulated
55951-56000	8-2 plug	Insulated
56001-56100	8-2 plug	Insulated
56101-56175	8-7 plug	Insulated
50-foot double door, 50-ton capacity		
3801-3862	15-0	
12002-12150	12-0	Steel frame. Staggered doors. To woodchip cars 12201-12220.
19201-19250	15-0	
19301-19450	15-0	
19601-19700	15-0	
35001-35182	15-0	
35201-35425	15-0	
35501-35625	15-0	
40001-40100	12-0	Staggered door. End doors.

STOCK CARS

Series	Door Opening	Remarks
40-foot single deck, 40-ton capacity		
75801-76232	5-9	Steel underframe
40-foot double deck, 40-ton capacity		
75101-75200	5-0	Steel underframe

Western Pacific Freight Equipment of the 1970s

BOX CARS

Series	Length	Capacity	Door	Remarks
1952	45-9	100,000	6-0	Cushion frame.
3011-3050	55-10	110,000	8-0	Cushion frame.
3071-3073	54-4	100,000	8-0	
3084-3089	54-4	100,000	15-0	
3091-3092	54-4	100,000	15-0	
3101-3105	57-11	143,000	10-6	
3151-3167	67-0	134,000	10-0	
3171-3187	67-0	182,000	10-0	
3201-3220	57-11	148,000	10-6	
3302	56-9	100,000	15-0	
3334-3369	56-1	110,000	8-0	
3401-3410	45-9	100,000	8-0	
3416-3417	44-2	100,000	9-0	Ex-Milwaukee Road.
3421-3422	44-4	100,000	8-0	
3423-3426	44-4	100,000	8-0	
3431-3435	44-9	110,000	8-0	Ex-Santa Fe.
3441-3442	44-4	100,000	8-0	Rblt 20891-21400.
3451-3472	44-4	100,000	7-0	
3701-3725	69-1	177,000	16-0	
3726-3736	68-2	163,000	16-0	
3737-3744	68-4	173,000	15-3	
3751-3754	70-11	200,000	16-0	Leased from N&W.
3761-3767	65-3	169,000	16-0	
3768-3775	67-9	169,000	16-0	
3789-3798	54-6	110,000	15-0	

BOX CARS (cont'd)

Series	Length	Capacity	Door	Remarks
3801-3837	54-4	100,000	15-0	
3838-3864	54-6	110,000	15-0	
3865-3950	54-6	98,000	15-0	
3965-3989	54-4	110,000	15-0	
3990-3995				Renumbered from 3001-3010.
3996	54-6	110,000	8-0	Renumbered from 36003.
3997-4006	56-1	110,000	8-0	Renumbered from 3011-3050.
4008	54-6	110,000	10-0	
4017	54-6	110,000	15-0	
4051-4060	57-10	143,000	10-0	
18501-18504	44-4	90,000	12-0	
18505	44-2	100,000	12-6	Converted from 20201 series.
18551	58-4	140,000	15-0	Converted from 35402.
18553	56-10	100,000	15-0	Converted from 35418.
18561-18563	58-5	100,000	8-0	
19301-19450	54-4	120,000	15-0	
19551-19560	44-4	100,000	7-0	
19601-19725	54-6	120,000	15-0	
19801-19850	54-6	154,000	10-0	

FLAT CARS

Series	Remarks
50-foot, 50-ton capacity	
2301-2350	Steel underframe
2351-2400	Steel frame, 2'6" high side boards, fixed ends, wood floor, sand and gravel service.
2401-2700	Steel underframe
2701-2802	Steel underframe
2851-2925	Bulkhead, 42'6" inside length.
55-foot, 50-ton capacity	
1901-1910	TOFC service.
2001-2050	
2201-2224	Auto parts service.
2951-2980	Wallboard service.

GONDOLAS

Series	Remarks
40-foot, 50-ton capacity	
4001-4061	Drop bottom, wood rack for woodchip service.
4101-4500	Drop bottom, 4301 equipped with wood rack.
5301-6000	Drop bottom
30-foot, 70-ton capacity	
6401-6500	Mill type, drop ends.
45-foot, 70-ton capacity	
9101-9400	Drop bottom
9401-9700	Drop bottom

GONDOLAS (cont'd)

Series	Remarks
55-foot, 70-ton capacity	
6501-6600	Low side, drop ends, wood floor.
6601-6800	Low side, drop ends, wood floor.
65-foot, 70-ton capacity	
9001-9050	Low side, drop ends, steel floor.

COVERED HOPPERS

Series	Remarks
11201-11210	70-ton, double hopper, 35'3" over strikers.
11301-11330	70-ton, double hopper, 35'3" over strikers.
14601-14602	50-ton, bulk sugar loading, 41'9" over strikers.

BALLAST CARS

Series	Remarks
10301-10600	50-ton, Hart selective, 31'9" over strikers.
10601-10700	70-ton, 31'9" over strikers.

WOODCHIP CARS

Series	Remarks
12201-12220	50-ton, 52'2" over strikers. Converted from 12001-12150 box cars.

TANK CARS

Series	Remarks
1201-1250	12,500 gallon, 42'2" over strikers.

Source: *Compiled from Western Pacific Freight Equipment records.*

BOX CARS (cont'd)

Series	Length	Capacity	Door	Remarks
19901-19902	56-9	140,000	14-5	
19951-19960	56-9	110,000	14-5	
20201-20550	44-3	100,000	6-0	
20551-20800	44-3	100,000	7-0	
20804-21400	44-4	131,000	7-0	
21513	44-4	131,000	7-0	
22001-22025	44-4	131,000	7-0	Converted from 20821-21400.
23001	45-9	110,000	8-0	
26001-26125	44-10	80,000	6-0	Steel underframe
27001-27600	44-6	80,000	6-0	Steel underframe
30001-30010	54-6	140,000	15-0	Conv 35401-35425.
34004-34023	54-4	110,000	15-0	
35001-35099	54-5	110,000	15-0	
35101-35400	54-6	100,000	15-0	
35401-35425	54-4	100,000	15-0	
35501-35625	54-4	100,000	15-0	
35701-35750	53-2	110,000	15-0	
36001-36025	54-4	100,000	8-0	
35801-35900	54-4	120,000	15-0	
36002-36050	54-6	124,000	8-0	
36102-36140	56-1	110,000	8-0	
37001-37200	54-4	158,000	10-6 plug	
38001-38225	57-2	154,000	16-0	
38226-38325	56-5	155,000	16-0	
39001-39010	58-10	145,000	14-0	
45001-45200	54-5	120,000	15-0	
55901-55920	53-2	100,000	7-7 plug	Insulated
55926-55950	54-4	100,000	8-7 plug	Insulated
55951-56000	54-8	94,000	8-2 plug	Insulated
56001-56100	54-9	97,000	8-2 plug	Insulated
56101-56175	54-4	100,000	8-7 plug	Insulated
56176-56325	54-11	140,000	9-0 plug	Insulated
57001-57100	54-4	107,000	10-0 plug	Insulated
59001-59025	54-4	140,000	8-7 plug	Insulated
59101-59125	54-4	140,000	8-7 plug	Insulated
59130-59131	53-8	140,000	9-2 plug	Insulated
60001-60050	56-3	124,000	9-0 plug	Insulated
60101-60290	57-8	147,000	9-0	Insulated
60291-60300	54-5	140,000	9-0 plug	Insulated
60301-60340	57-1	147,000	9-0 plug	Insulated
60405	58-10	143,000	9-2	
60411-60440	58-2	143,000	9-2	
60501-60514	57-6	145,000	10-0 plug	Insulated
60521-60525	57-8	140,000	12-0 plug	Insulated
60526-60535	57-8	140,000	10-0 plug	Insulated
60601-60650	58-1	140,000	15-0 plug	Insulated
60651-60800	58-2	140,000	15-0 plug	Insulated
60801-60814	58-6	139,000	10-0 plug	Insulated
60815-60850	57-8	140,000	10-0 plug	Insulated
60851-60950	57-8	140,000	10-0 plug	
61001-61050	54-11	151,000	14-6 plug	Insulated
61051-61086	58-0	146,000	16-0 plug	Insulated
61091-61092	58-2	145,000	15-0 plug	Insulated
61101-61296	54-9	146,000	10-6 plug	Insulated
62001-62225	58-3	142,000	15-0 plug	Insulated
64001-64074	58-2	176,000	15-0 plug	Insulated
64501-64575	57-1	143,000	14-0 plug	Insulated
64701-64748	56-9	134,000	14-0 plug	Insulated
64801-64934	58-10	145,000	14-0 plug	Insulated
64951-64995	58-0	147,000	14-0 plug	Insulated
65001-65111	56-3	142,000	10-6 plug	Insulated
65201-65400	60-6	137,000	15-0 plug	Insulated
65401-65600	60-6	137,000	15-0 plug	Insulated
66001-66050	67-9	134,000	15-0 plug	Insulated
66101-66200	69-6	170,000	10-6 plug	Insulated
66501-66550	67-9	168,000	15-0 plug	Insulated
67001-67006	68-6	150,000	10-0 plug	Insulated
67007-67019	68-2	162,000	10-6 plug	Insulated
67020-67041	67-10	164,000	10-0 plug	Insulated
67042-67051	68-6	163,000	10-6 plug	Insulated
67052-67055	70-0	167,000	12-0 plug	Insulated
68001-68225	58-1	143,000	15-0 plug	Insulated
68226-68325	58-2	142,000	10-6 plug	Insulated
68501-68543	58-2	143,000	15-0 plug	Insulated

BOX CARS (cont'd)

Series	Length	Capacity	Door	Remarks
68601-68766	58-2	143,000	15-0 plug	Insulated
86002-86035	93-9	104,000	20-0 plug	
86036-86041	93-11	142,000	20-0 plug	
86042-86077	93-11	144,000	20-0 plug	
86078-86102	92-10	151,000	20-0 plug	
86103-86127	92-10	148,000	20-0 plug	
92264-92288	58-4	138,000	10-1 plug	Insulated
95951-95967	58-5	139,000	10-1 plug	Insulated
96043-96118	58-4	138,000	12-6 plug	Insulated
98093-98096	58-4	140,000	10-6 plug	Insulated
960854-960861	67-4	169,000	16-0 plug	
960862-960876	68-2	143,000	16-0 plug	

FLAT CARS

Series	Length	Capacity	Door	Remarks
1101-1124	90-7	135,000		Containers
1401-1410	68-0	198,000		Center Beam
1451-1490	70-6	186,000		Bulkhead
1601-1602	81-1	300,000		Depressed center
1611-1630	89-11	100,000		Flexi-Van
1701-1725	88-2	135,000		TOFC
1752	53-3	110,000		
1811-1815	54-1	195,000		Rocket motors
1816-1820	54-1	189,000		Transformers
1834	106-6	220,000		Twin-unit car
1841-1850	64-6	154,000		
1851-1865	107-3	220,000		Twin-unit car
1866-1868	109-5	220,000		Twin-unit car
1881-1898	106-6	220,000		Twin-unit car
1901	93-9	130,000		
1902-1910	59-3	100,000		TOFC: two 24' or one 35'+ trailer; converted from 2001-2050 series.
1926-1941	53-3	100,000		TOFC: one 40' trailer; converted from 2701-2802 series.
2090-2099	59-3	110,000		
2101-2150	59-3	140,000		
2151-2159	64-6	140,000		
2160	64-6	154,000		
2161-2175	65-2	160,000		
2201-2224	56-9	110,000		
2226-2230	59-3	165,000		Transformers
2231-2250	56-9	127,000		
2351-2400	53-3	100,000		30" side boards.
2401-2700	53-3	100,000		
2701-2802	53-3	110,000		
2817-2819	59-3	140,000		Bulkhead, converted from 2101-2150 series.
2820-2825	59-3	100,000		Bulkhead
2826-2840	59-3	140,000		Bulkhead
2841-2850	59-3	140,000		Bulkhead, converted from 2101-2050 series.
2851-2925	53-3	100,000		Bulkhead
2926-2930	59-3	154,000		Bulkhead
2931-2950	59-3	100,000		Bulkhead, converted from 2051-2075 series.
2951-2989	59-3	100,000		Bulkhead, converted from 2001-2050 series.
2990	59-3	100,000		Bulkhead, converted from 2931-2950 series.
2991-3000	59-3	140,000		Bulkhead, converted from 2101-2150 series.
8801-9000	94-8	140,000		TOFC
13101-13150	64-6	140,000		Bulkhead
13201-13217	53-3	110,000		

FLAT CARS (cont'd)

Series	Length	Capacity	Remarks
13301-13307	118-6	230,000	Twin-unit car for two 20' COFC.
259100-259299	56-9	154,000	Steel coil

GONDOLAS

Series	Length	Capacity	Remarks
4401-4425	34-6	172,000	Steel coil
5001-5070	49-9	156,000	Wood rack, drop bottom for wood chip service.
5101-5112	64-8	192,000	Woodchip
6001-6002	57-1	140,000	Covered
6011-6015	56-11	187,000	Covered, steel service.
6051-6060	57-7	156,000	Covered
6061-6062	70-5	135,000	Covered
6063-6064	57-7	137,000	Covered
6201-6210	34-0	211,000	Ex-Oro Dam
6300-6400	57-7	140,000	Steel coil
6401-6500	33-5	140,000	Steel coil
6501-6600	57-7	160,000	Steel coil
6601-6800	57-7	160,000	
6801-6850	57-2	140,000	
6901-6925	50-6	140,000	Converted from 9401-9700 series.
6926-7082	50-6	162,000	
7701-7740	57-1	188,000	
9001-9050	70-5	140,000	Hot steel billets
9051-9065	69-8	187,000	Hot steel billets
9101-9400	49-9	144,000	Drop bottom
9401-9700	50-6	140,000	Drop bottom
9701-9775	49-9	140,000	Drop bottom
9776-9793	49-9	162,000	Drop bottom
99101-99133	49-9	166,000	Drop bottom, renumbered from 9101-9400 series.
99134-99188	50-6	165,000	Drop bottom, renumbered from 9401-9700 series.
99189-99200	49-9	140,000	Drop bottom, renumbered from 9701-9775 series.
99201-99239	49-9	162,000	Drop bottom

WOODCHIP CARS

Series	Length	Capacity	Remarks
5101-5112	63-8	192,000	
12201-12220	54-5	100,000	Rebuilt from box cars.

COVERED HOPPERS

Series	Length	Capacity	Remarks
4700-4724	41-3	200,000	Leased from Chicago Freight Car Leasing (CRDX reporting marks).

COVERED HOPPERS (cont'd)

Series	Length	Capacity	Remarks
11201-11210	37-9	140,000	
11301-11300	37-9	140,000	
11501-11510	49-7	158,000	
11526-11534	49-7	155,000	
11536-11545	49-7	156,000	
11551-11559	49-7	156,000	
11601-11616	42-0	140,000	Single Airslide™
11617-11662	42-1	140,000	Single Airslide™
11671-11685	53-4	188,000	Double Airslide™
11686-11690	53-11	190,000	Double Airslide™
11701-11712	49-2	196,000	Stainless steel quad
11713	51-6	200,000	Stainless steel triple
11741-11750	59-1	217,000	3-bay CenterFlow™
11751-11800	54-6	198,000	3-bay CenterFlow™
11801-11825	53-10	196,000	3-bay CenterFlow™
11826-11850	54-6	196,000	
11851-11900	57-7	207,000	
11901-11965	54-6	197,000	CenterFlow™
11966-12000	57-11	198,000	CenterFlow™
12001-12050	54-6	197,000	CenterFlow™
12051-12100	57-9	197,000	
30060,30062, 30064-30067	41-1	140,000	SHPX (Shipper's Car Line).
60300-60309		140,000	NIHX, single Airslide™.
92001-92017	51-6	200,000	NIHX, stainless steel triple.

OPEN HOPPERS

Series	Length	Capacity	Remarks
10001-10050	42-3	205,000	Ballast
10086-10200	44-5	203,000	
10201-10230	43-9	205,000	
10231-10295	44-5	200,000	
10301-10575	38-10	200,000	
10601-10700	34-3	172,000	Ballast
10701-10800	35-1	171,000	Ballast
10800-11000	42-10	200,000	
38700-38714	53-1	197,000	
41400-41499	51-8	200,000	
70000-70240	53-1	200,000	See photo page 127

TANK CARS

Series	Length	Capacity	Remarks
1201-1250	44-8		12,500 gallon, single dome.
1301-1359	34-10		10,040 gallon, single dome.
1361-1371	35-6		10,040 gallon, single dome.

Source: *Compiled from Western Pacific Freight Equipment records.*

Chapter 4 Endnotes

1 Western Pacific Mechancial Records

5 Work Equipment

(above) WP 40-foot PS-1 box car MW0242, converted to work service. *(John Ryczkowski)*

(left) Still another 40-foot PS-1 assigned to maintenance of way service, MW0223 illustrates a further variation in WP box car lettering. *(John Ryczkowski)*

Work equipment not only plays a vital role in the maintenance of a railroad company, but much of this equipment is an "extended life" operation of former revenue freight or passenger cars. Consequently, by the study of both diagrams and photos of work equipment, it is possible to get a good idea of what the cars looked like during their revenue service. Granted, the numbers, paint schemes, and overall appearances may have been changed, but the clues are often still there. Hopefully, this chapter will provide some basic information about WP equipment not otherwise obtainable.

Work equipment can generally be divided into two classifications. First, there is the equipment that is purchased new for specific types of work, such as snow plows, Jordan Spreaders, and wreckers; then the equipment rebuilt from former revenue box cars, refrigerator cars, gondolas, flat cars, and passenger equipment.

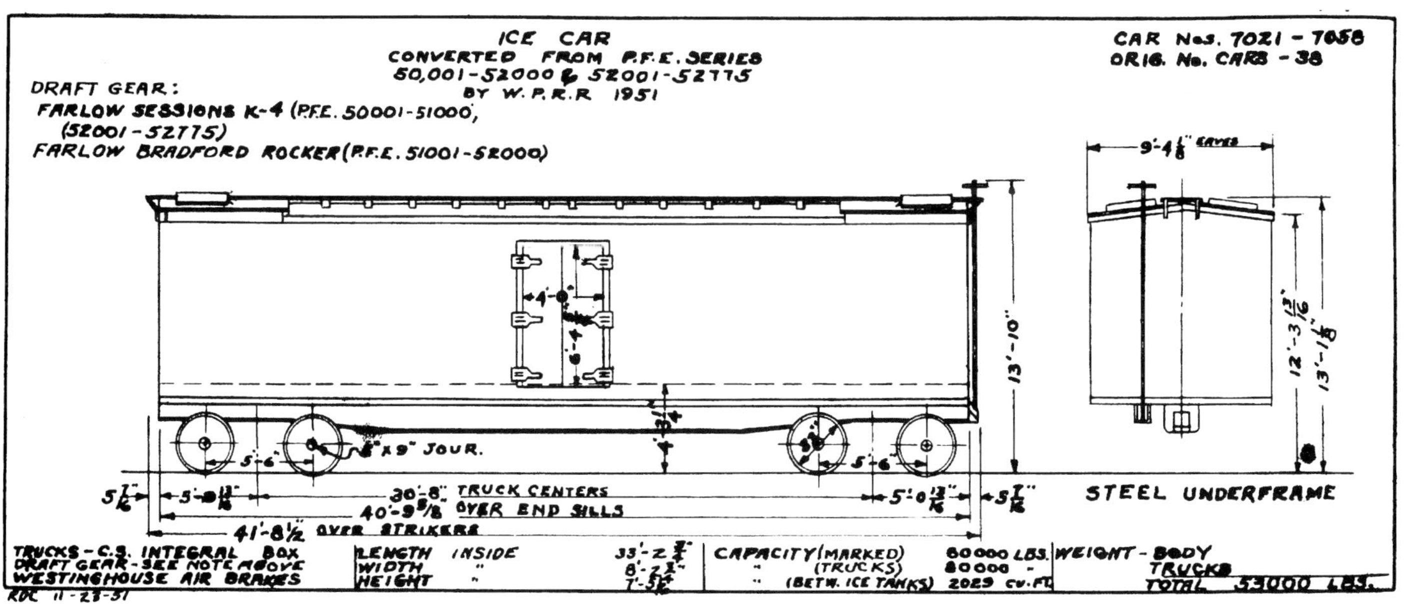

What happened to some of the former Pacific Fruit Express (PFE) wooden refrigerator cars? Repainted silver, the cars went into "Ice Service" in 1954. MW7034's original PFE number, 51563, is still visible on the end! Photographed at Portola in 1969. *(Bob Larson)*

Spreader number 8 was seen at Portola in 1964. *(Bob Larson)*

Western Pacific Work Equipment Summary

Type	Series	Length	Remarks
Rotary Snow Plow	3	41-10	
Rotary Snow Plow	4	40-7	
Jordan Spreaders	6-7	52-6	
Dirt Dozer	8	44-1	
Jordan Spreaders	10-11	37-10	Ditching service.
Jordan Spreader	13	50-6	
Weed Killer Spray Car	14	44-10	
Flat Cars	15-16	43-0	Used with off-track shovels.
Tender Cars	27, 28, 37	31-10	Used with Derricks 27, 28, 37.
Crane	36	27-10	
Wrecker	37	39-11	
Boom Idler Car	38	44-6	
Boom Car	39		
Boom Idler Cars	40, 41	44-6	
Truck and Block Car	42	44-10	
Flat Car	49	29-6	
Flat Car	50	42-11	Used with off-track shovels.
Crane Tender	53	29-4	
Locomotive Crane	54	29-4	
Burro Crane	B-64	12-6	
Boom Idler/Truck Car	76	40-7	
Diesel Water Tenders	81, 82	48-8	Rotary snow plow service.
Locomotive Crane	89	28-1	
Locomotive Crane	90	29-4	
100-ton Derricks	27, 28	28-8	
Boom Idler Car	39	44-10	Used with Wrecker 27.
Boat Flat Cars	150-153	40-7	Idler cars for car ferry switching.
Tank Cars	1001-1010	35-6	
Tank Cars	1021-1080	35-6	
Sand Cars	1023, 1028, 1035, 1038, 1048	35-6	Rebuilt from tank cars.
Tank Cars	1081-1180	34-10	10,400 gallons, car oil or weed killer service.
Solution Cars	1138, 1144		Weed killer service.
Water Cars	1501-1750	various	
Flat Car	2349	53-3	Off-track equipment.
Gondolas	6101-6131	44-6	Low sides, rebuilt from 16001-18500 box cars.
Ice Cars	7011-7020	44-4	Steel underframe.
Ice Cars	7021-7058	43-3	
Tie Cars	7503-7519	53-3	Converted from 2301-2350 flats.

Type	Series	Length	Remarks
Pile Driver Tender	8004	35-6	Converted from tank 1058.
Diesel Oil Peddler Car	8022	43-5	Converted from box 16701.
Stores Box Cars	8051-8085	44-10	Steel underframe.
Wheel Cars	8501-8510	44-6	
Flat Cars	8511, 8513	44-6	Waste and material service.
Traction Motor Car	8512	44-6	
Flat Cars	8514-8530	44-6	
Combination Gon-Flats	8531-8549	40-7	
Low-side Gondolas	8550, 8551	40-7	Stores service.
Low-side Gondolas	8552-8555	40-7	Loose wheel load ing, rebuilt from 75501-75800 stock cars.
Leader Idler Car	8556	40-7	Used with Pile Driver 70.
Leader Idler Car	8557	53-3	Used with Pile Driver 90.
Main Generator/ TractionMotor Car	8558	43-0	
Flat Car	8560	53-6	Equipped with "Binanbatch" for tunnel lining operations.
Dump Cars	11001-11040	40-0	
Outfit Cars	01-0500		
Tender Flat Car	MW0312	44-6	Used with Wrecker 37.
Rail and Tie Car	MW 0313X	44-6	Used with Wrecker 37.
Outfit Cars	0501-0800		
Rail and Tie Car	MW 0628X	44-10	
Truck and Block Car	MW0633	44-10	
Engine/Trainmens' Car	0751-X2	44-5	
Engine/Trainmens' Car	0752-X3	43-9	
Tool and Water Cars	MW0941TW MW0942TW	40-7	
Ventilated Tool Car	09517-09977	40-7	Converted from 75501-75800 stock cars.
Emergency Tool Cars	0579T, 0584T, 0635T, 0674T, 0675T, 0703T, 0704T, 0705T	44-10	
Bunk Cars	0901-0910		
Kitchen-Dining Car	0911-0915		
Kitchen-Dining Car	0916-0917		

Note: This is a representative summary of WP work equipment, rather than a comprehensive roster.

Source: *Western Pacific Work Equipment Records.*

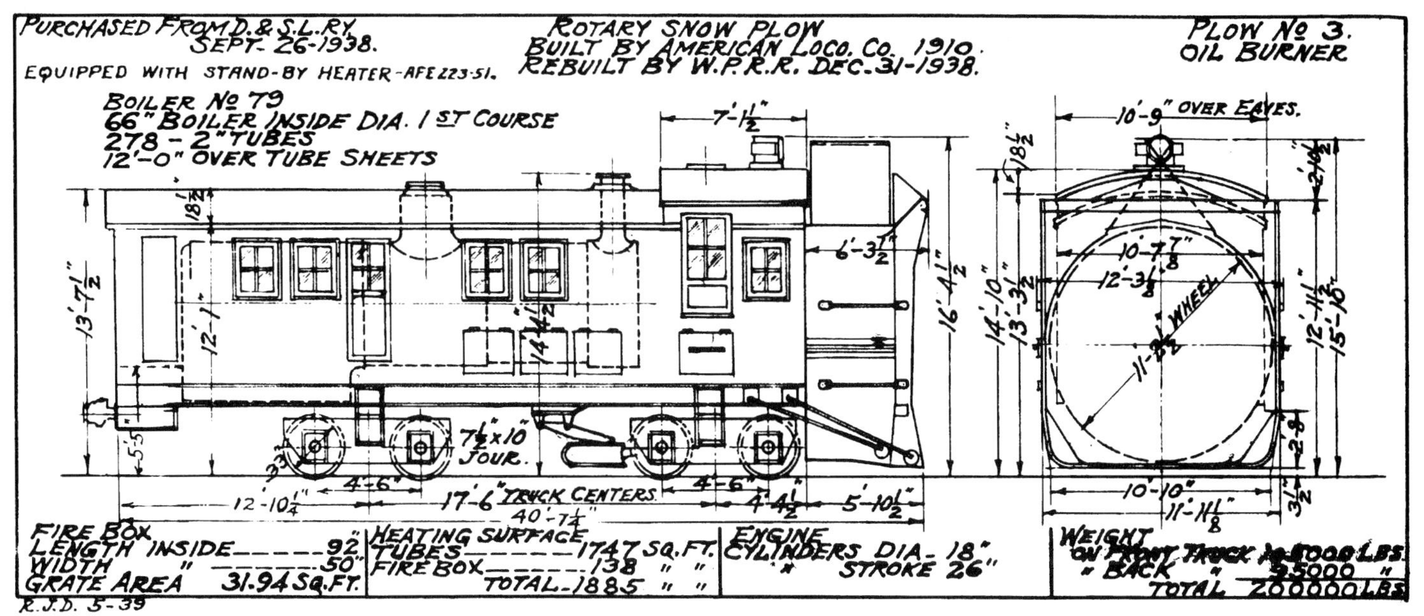

(left) Rotary snowplow MW Rotary 3, ready for service at Portola in 1964.

(Bob Larson)

(right) Rotary snowplow number 4 was photographed at Portola in 1963.

(Bob Larson)

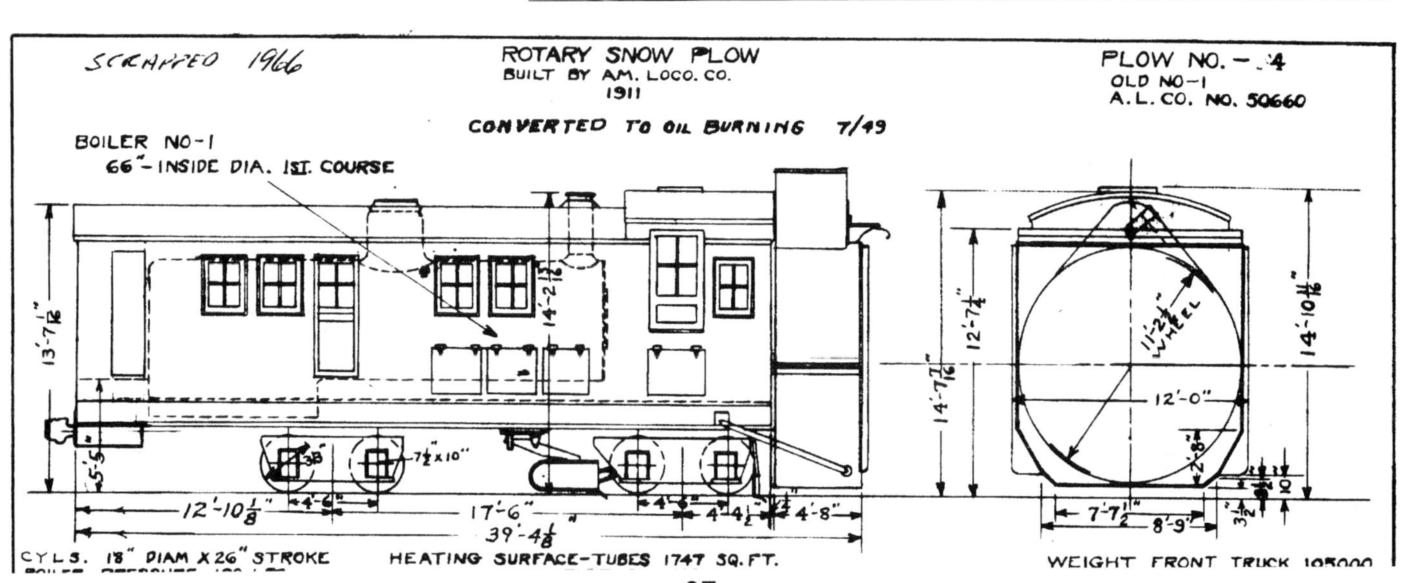

Western Pacific wrecker 27 and boom car MW 39 at Portola, California, in 1964.
(Bob Larson)

Wrecker 28 at Portola on the Elko hook crew, September 3, 1971.
(Bob Larson)

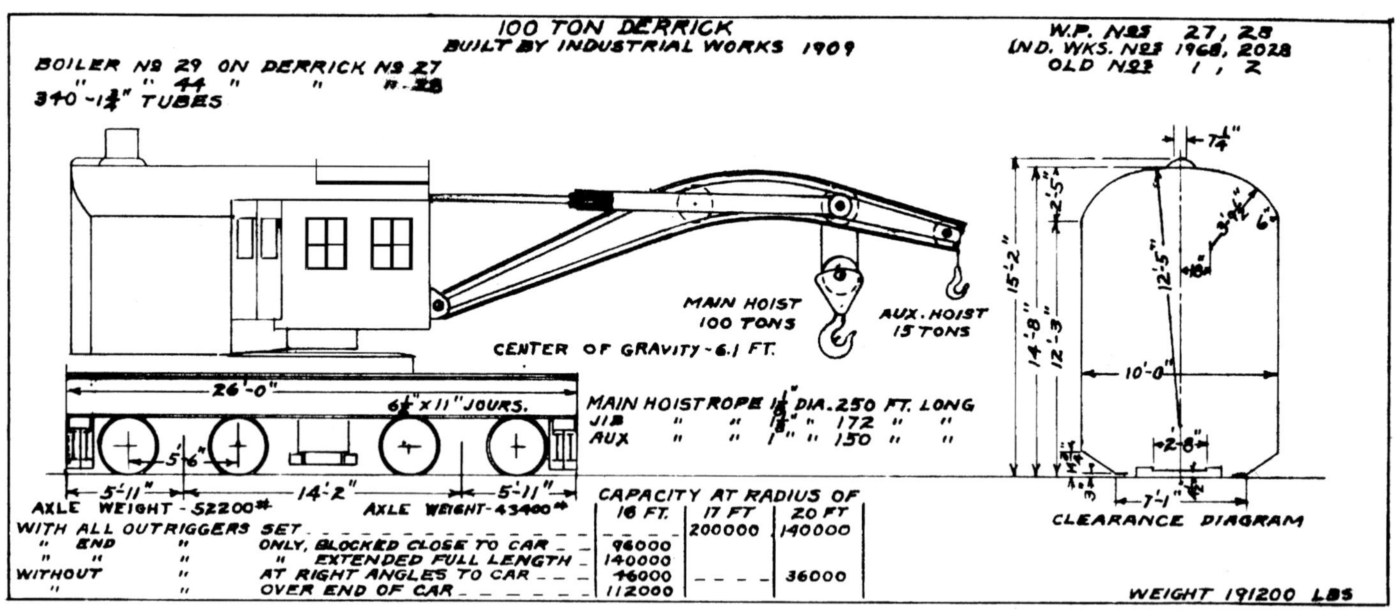

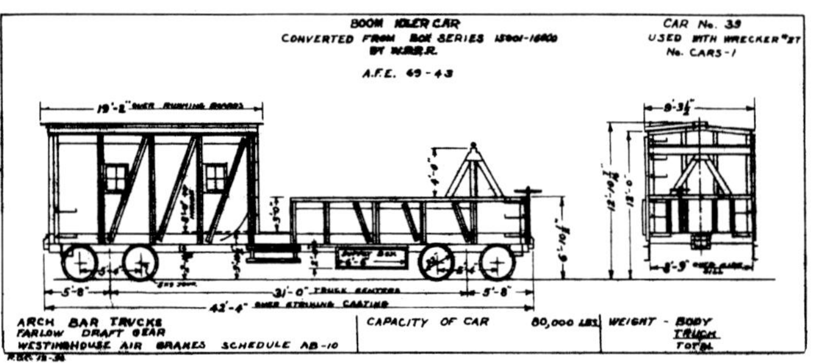

(above) Diagram of boom idler car 39.
(Western Pacific Railroad, Collection of the Author)

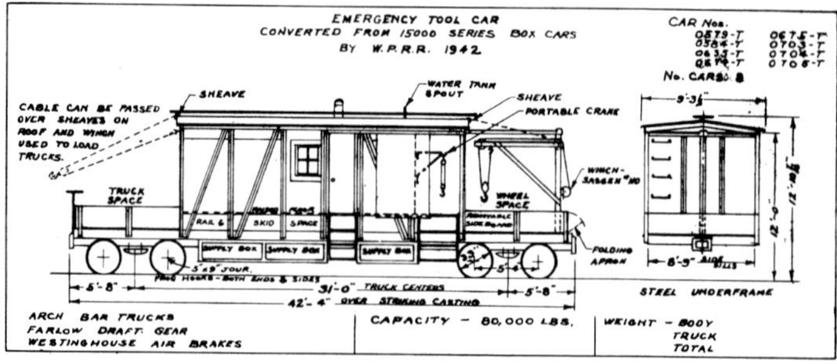

(above) Diagram of tool and wheel cars.
(Western Pacific Railroad, Collection of the Author)

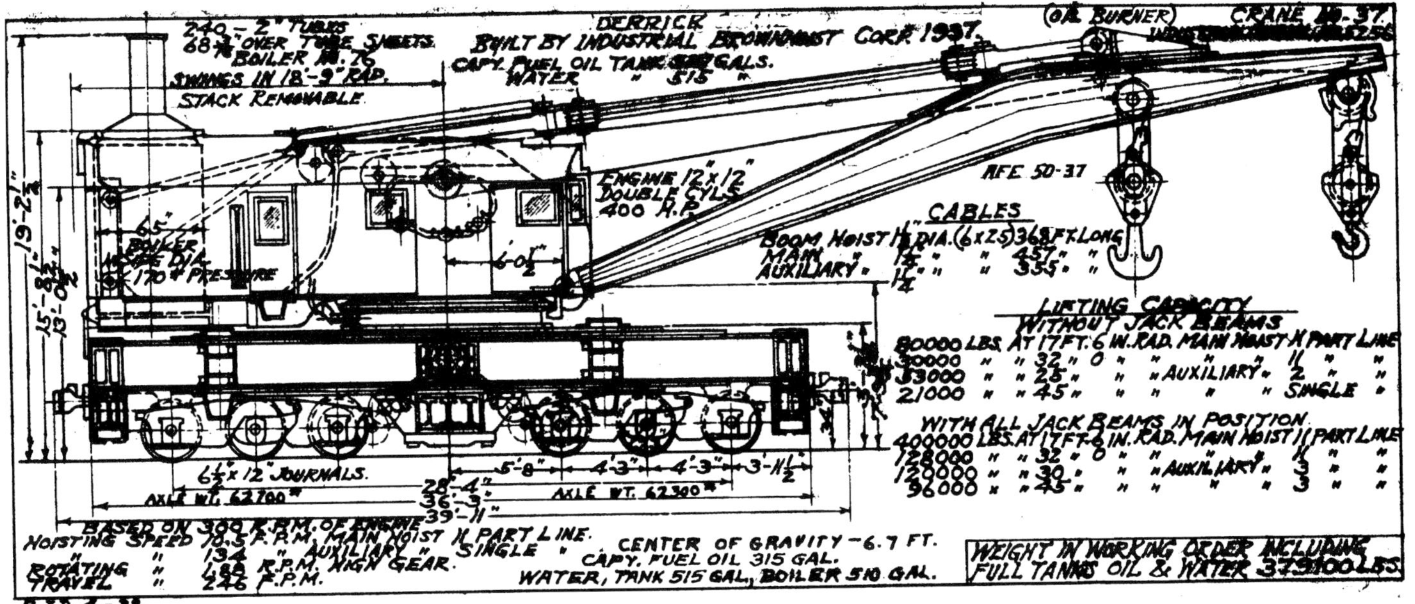

Wrecker 37 at Portola, California, shortly after being built by Industrial Brownhoist Corporation in 1937.
(Bob Larson Collection)

Crane tender 53 at Oakland on January 27, 1946.
(Bob Larson Collection)

Tool and Wheel Car MW0584 at Oakland on May 10, 1938.
(Bob Larson Collection)

Western Pacific converted a group of tank cars into dry sand service, such as MW1035 seen at Portola in September 1972.
(Bob Larson)

Dry sand car MW1048 at Oakland, California, on April 11, 1968.
(Collection of Howard W. Ameling)

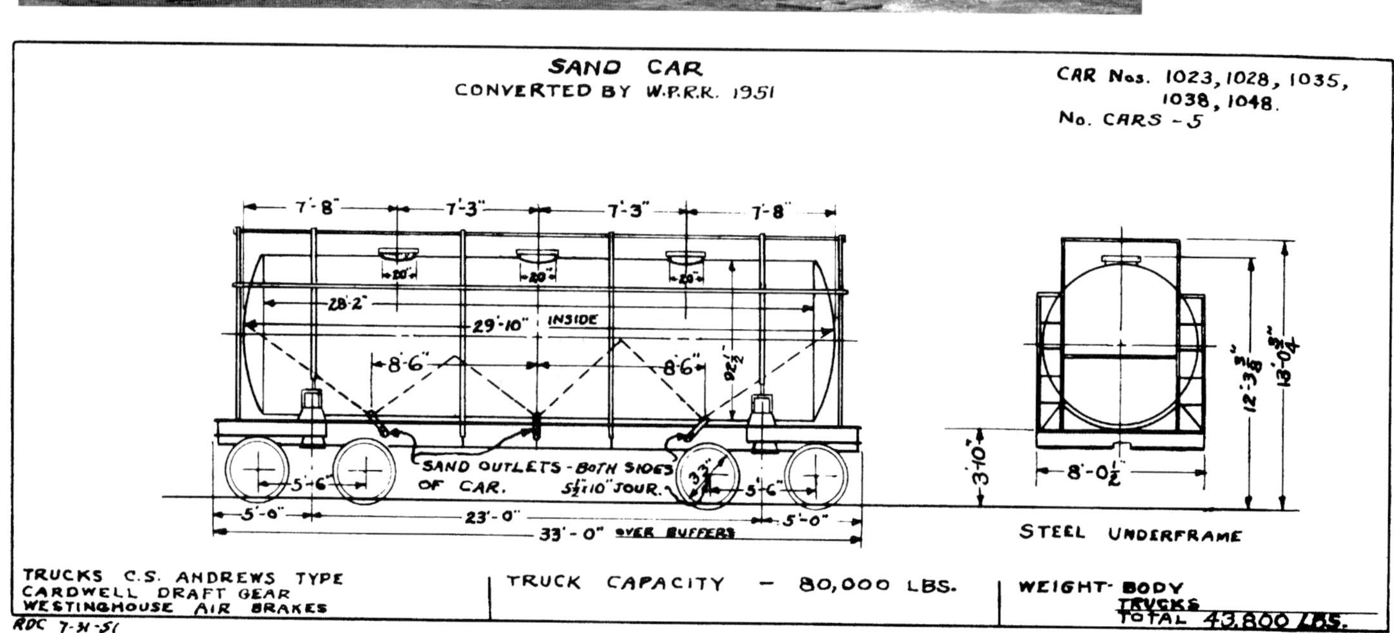

(above) Combination kitchen-dining car MW0915-CD was converted to work car service at the Sacramento Shops in June 1953. Photographed at Oakland, California, on September 23, 1967.
(Collection of Howard W. Ameling)

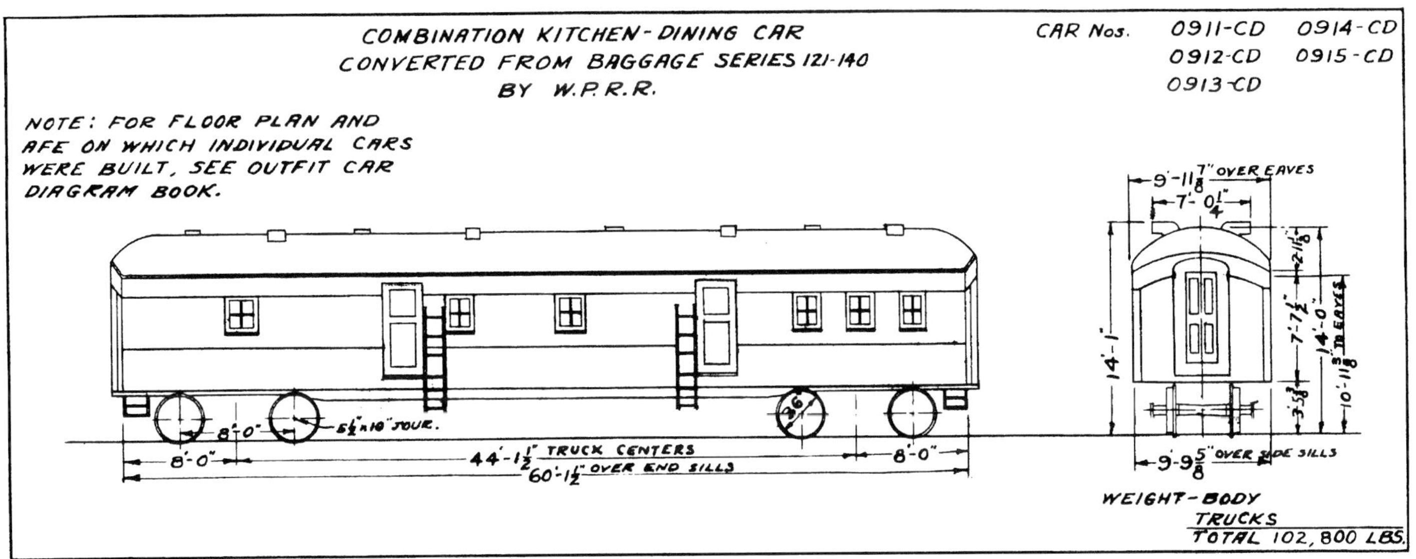

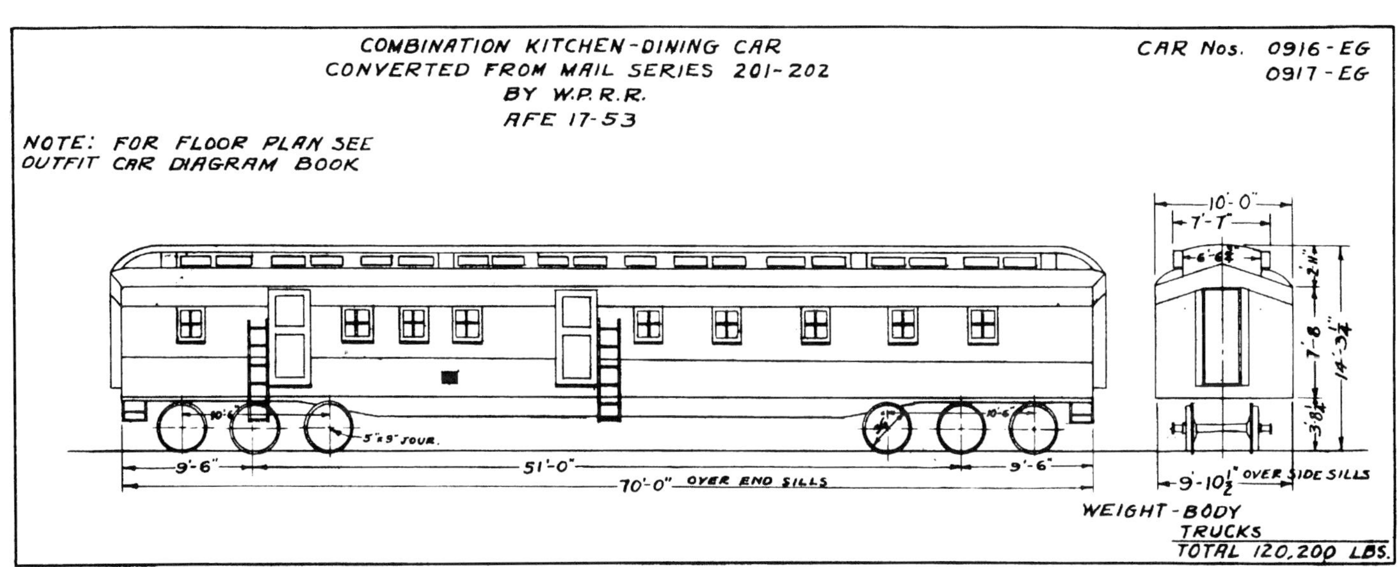

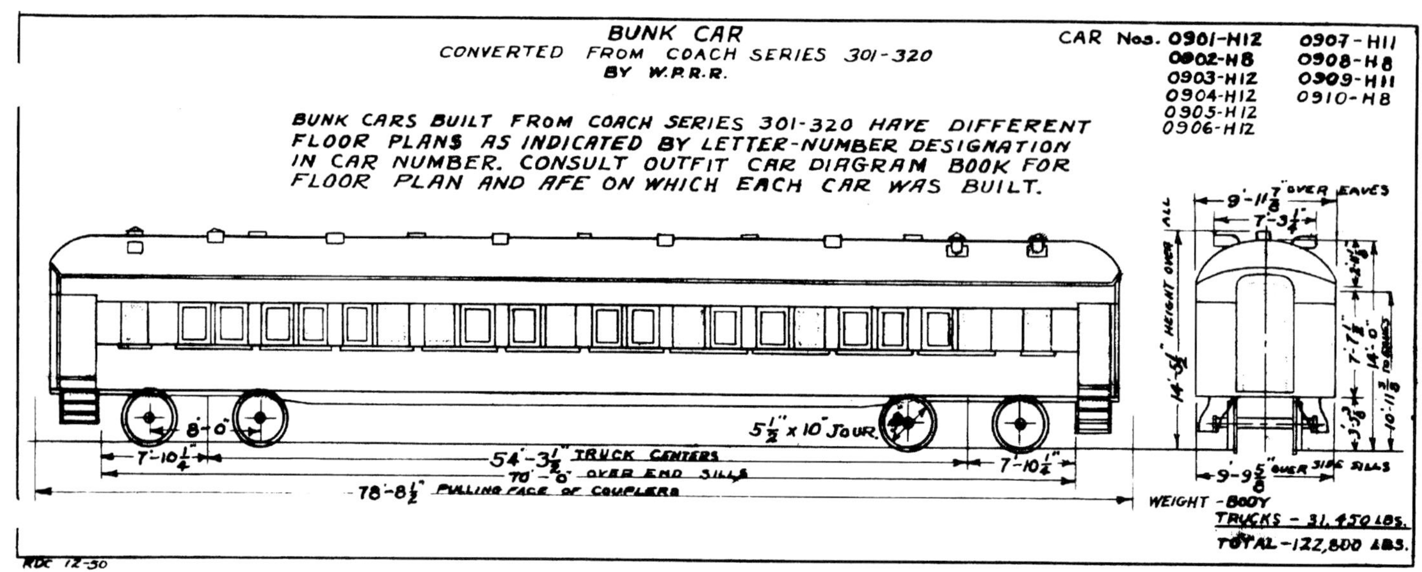

(above) One can learn a great deal about historical passenger equipment by studying those cars which have been converted to work or bunk car service, such as illustrated with this diagram of WP bunk cars rebuilt from coaches.

(Western Pacific Railroad, Collection of the Author)

(facing page, top) Weed sprayer MW14 is an example of a work car rebuilt from an outside braced wooden box car. The diagram indicates that the car was rebuilt from one of the 15001-16000 series box cars. The weed sprayer with its tanks cars 1138 and 144 was photographed between operations at Oakland, California, on August 27, 1966.

(Collection of Howard W. Ameling)

(below) Perhaps the most typical work cars were those rebuilt from old wooden box cars. WP MW 0771 M4 was such a rebuild and was serving the company at Milpitas, California, when photographed on March 30, 1969.

(Collection of Howard W. Ameling)

W P
MW-14

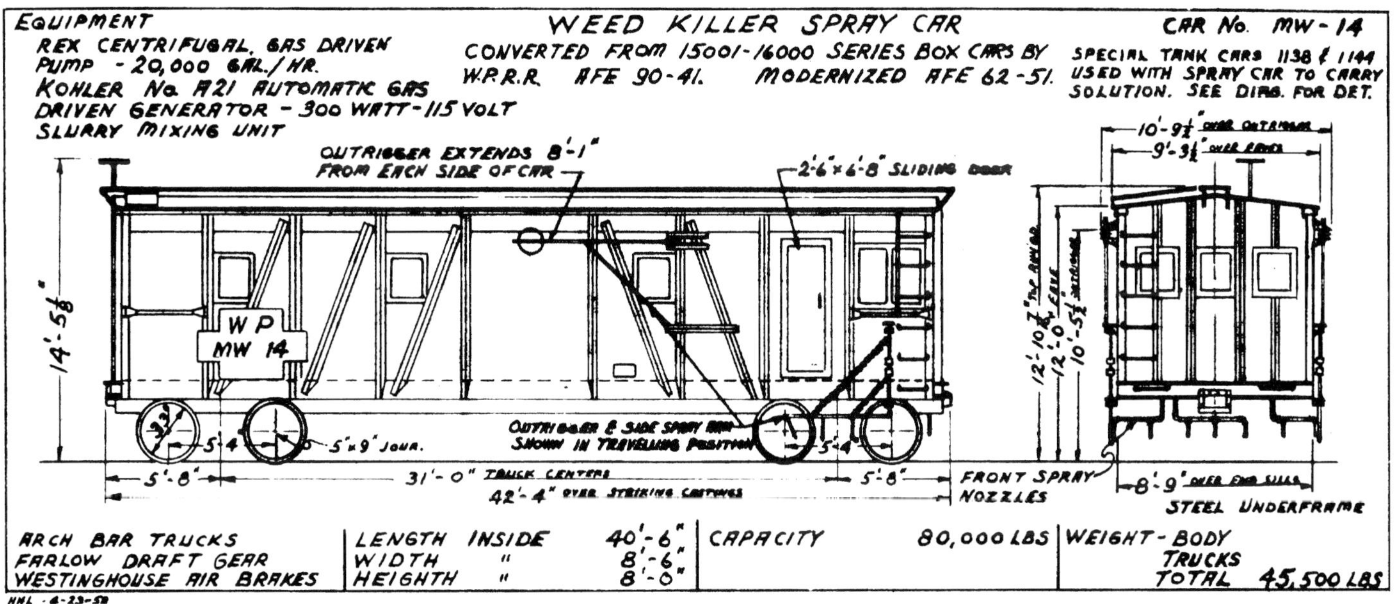

EQUIPMENT
REX CENTRIFUGAL, GAS DRIVEN PUMP - 20,000 GAL./HR.
KOHLER No. A21 AUTOMATIC GAS DRIVEN GENERATOR - 300 WATT - 115 VOLT
SLURRY MIXING UNIT
WEED KILLER SPRAY CAR
CONVERTED FROM 15001-16000 SERIES BOX CARS BY W.P.R.R. AFE 90-41. MODERNIZED AFE 62-51.
CAR No. MW-14
SPECIAL TANK CARS 1138 & 1144 USED WITH SPRAY CAR TO CARRY SOLUTION. SEE DIAG. FOR DET.
OUTRIGGER EXTENDS 8'-1" FROM EACH SIDE OF CAR
2'-6" x 6'-8" SLIDING DOOR
W P
MW 14
14'-5 5/8"
5'-4
5" x 9" JOUR.
OUTRIGGER & SIDE SPRAY ARM SHOWN IN TRAVELLING POSITION
5'-8"
31'-0" TRUCK CENTERS
42'-4" OVER STRIKING CASTINGS
FRONT SPRAY NOZZLES
10'-9 1/2" OVER OUTRIGGER
9'-3 1/2" OVER EAVES
12'-10 7/8"
12'-0" EAVE
10'-5 1/2"
8'-9" OVER END SILLS
STEEL UNDERFRAME
ARCH BAR TRUCKS
FARLOW DRAFT GEAR
WESTINGHOUSE AIR BRAKES
LENGTH INSIDE 40'-6"
WIDTH " 8'-6"
HEIGHTH " 8'-0"
CAPACITY 80,000 LBS
WEIGHT - BODY
TRUCKS
TOTAL 45,500 LBS
HHL - 6-23-58

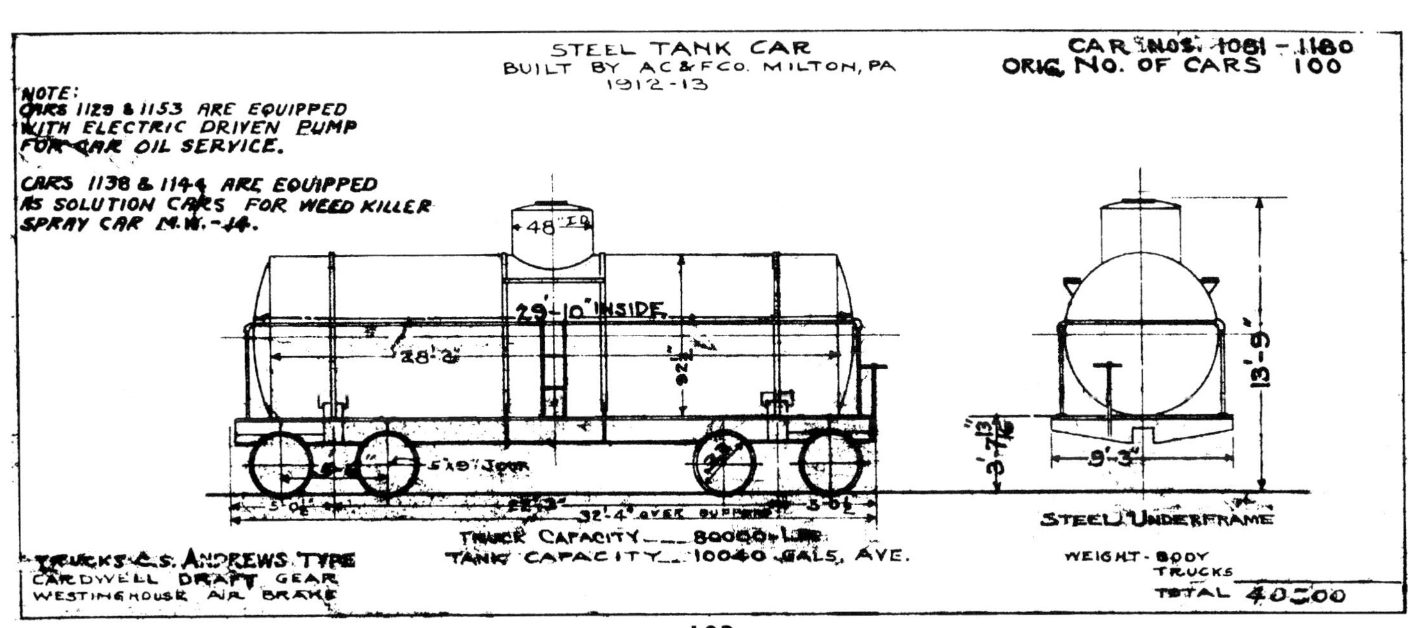

STEEL TANK CAR
BUILT BY AC&FCO. MILTON, PA
1912-13
CAR NOS. 1081 - 1180
ORIG. No. OF CARS 100
NOTE:
CARS 1129 & 1153 ARE EQUIPPED WITH ELECTRIC DRIVEN PUMP FOR CAR OIL SERVICE.
CARS 1138 & 1144 ARE EQUIPPED AS SOLUTION CARS FOR WEED KILLER SPRAY CAR M.W.-14.
48"
29'-10" INSIDE
28'-3"
5'x9" JOUR.
32'-4" OVER BUFFERS
13'-9"
9'-3"
STEEL UNDERFRAME
TRUCK CAPACITY___80000 LBS
TANK CAPACITY___10040 GALS. AVE.
TRUCKS C.S. ANDREWS TYPE
CARDWELL DRAFT GEAR
WESTINGHOUSE AIR BRAKE
WEIGHT - BODY
TRUCKS
TOTAL 40500

6 Cabooses

The caboose – the car that has punctuated the "end of the train" for nearly 160 years in North America – has been one of the most fascinating cars in the freight equipment category. The caboose has always seemed to mean more than just the "end of the train," carrying with it a mystique that is part of railroading's appeal.

The Western Pacific operated a superb fleet of cabooses, and a wide variety for the size of the railroad. This chapter illustrates the cars and color schemes in Western Pacific service. The final appearance of WP cabooses as part of the "UP" with Western Pacific lettering is covered in Chapter 7.

(top) Western Pacific caboose 446 was repainted and completely rebuilt in 1982 – note the silver roof and the striping on the ends of the car as well as on the bay window.

(John Ryczkowski)

(above) WP 441 was photographed in 1986 at the Chicago and North Western's Itasca Yard in Superior, Wisconsin. The caboose was in ore pool service.

(Bob Blomquist)

Western Pacific 437 was part of a 35-car fleet numbered 426 to 460. For the opposite side view, and still another lettering scheme, see photo of car 441 on opposite page.
(John Ryczkowski)

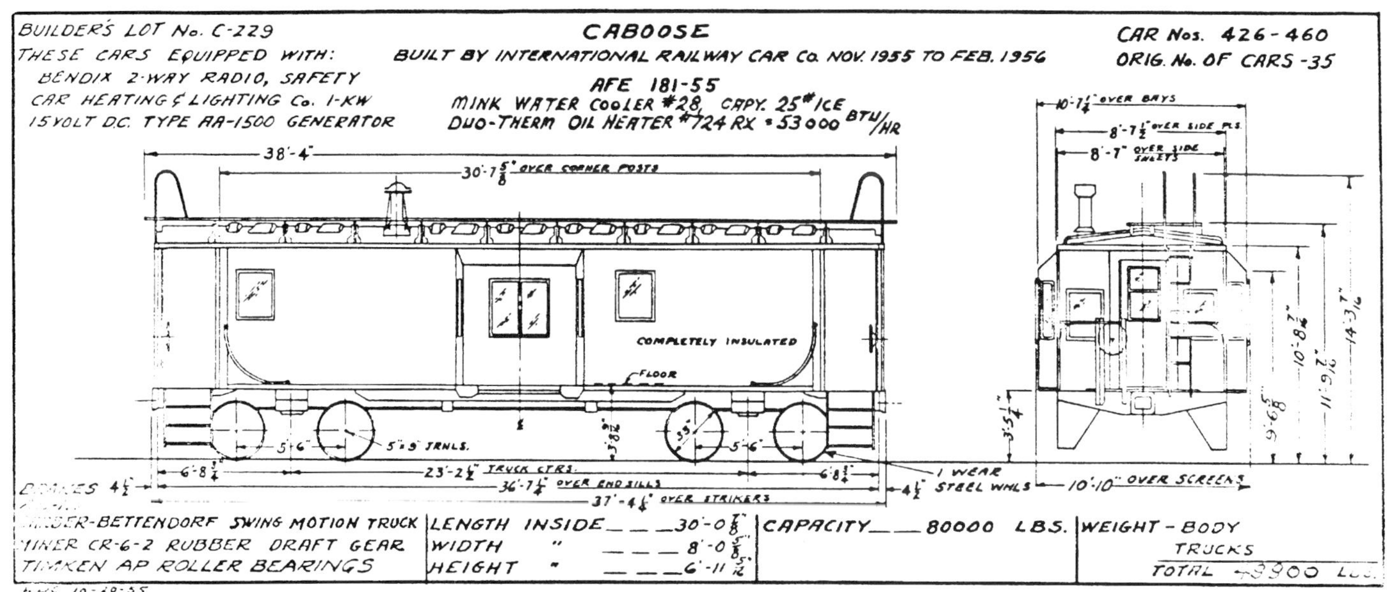

(above) Diagram of WP caboose series 426 to 460.
(Western Pacific Railroad, Collection of the Author)

(right) Caboose 444 illustrates still another lettering and paint application. It was photographed in service at Winnemucca, Nevada, in October 1979.
(Bob Larson)

Steel Cars

(above and left) Cabooses 429 and 451 illustrate the opposite sides of this series near the end of their careers on the Western Pacific and Union Pacific System. Council Bluffs, Iowa, 1989.

(Both Photos George R. Cockle, Collection of Howard W. Ameling)

(left) One final view of the 426 to 460 group. Car 458 is seen in service at Salt Lake City in the original lettering arrangement.

(Bob Larson)

(below) Caboose 473 (series 466 - 475) was constructed in 1973 and originally carried the Roman lettering.

(John Ryczkowski)

(above) The next group of cabooses, number series 476 to 480, were built in 1974. Note the small marker lights and and day-time marker flags on the upper corners of car 480. *(John Ryczkowski)*

(right) The final group of WP cabooses was built in 1980, such as the 483 seen in ore service on the C&NW at Superior, Wisconsin, in 1986. *(Author's Collection)*

(right) Caboose 485, also built in 1980, at Council Bluffs, Iowa, on December 2, 1988. *(Collection of Howard W. Ameling)*

Wooden Cars

(above) 625 was one of the many older cabooses painted in the orange and silver scheme during the latter part of their careers. Seen at Oakland in June 1961.

(Bob Larson)

(left) Wood bay window caboose 653. See diagram below for various number series. Salt Lake City, 1966.

(Bob Larson)

(below) Diagram of wood bay window cabooses 643-700, converted from box cars.

(Western Pacific Railroad, Collection of the Author)

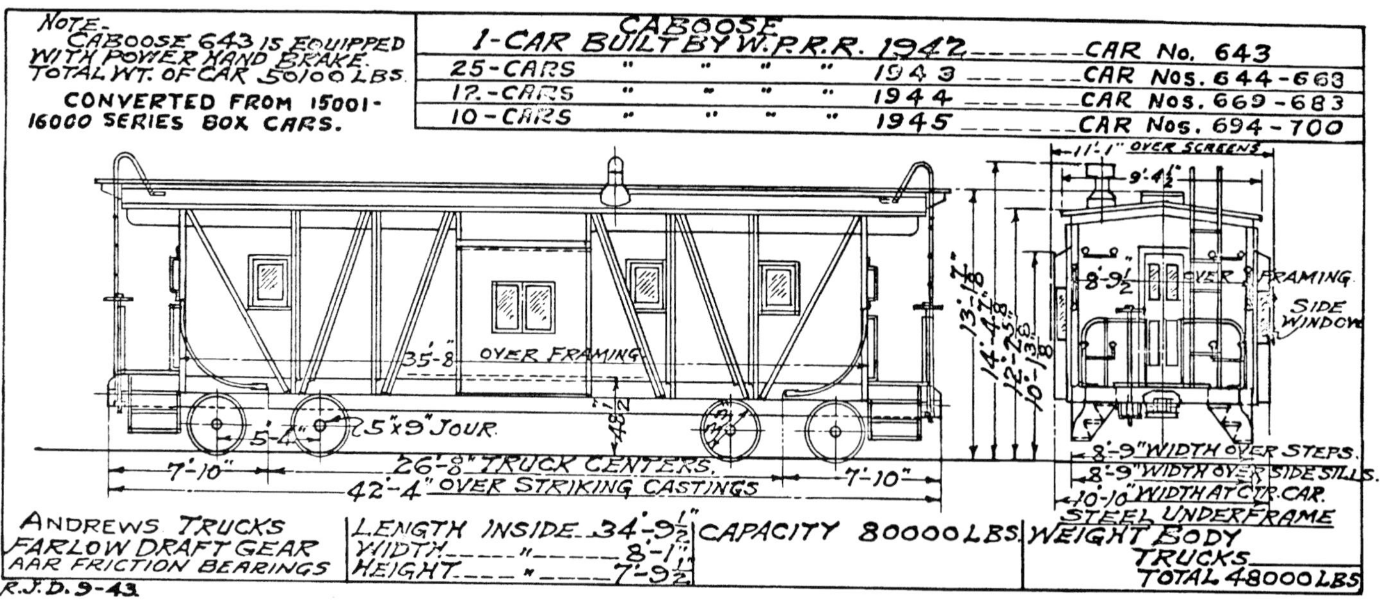

(top) Wood cupola caboose 726 painted in the orange and silver scheme. Seen in service at San Jose in November 1955.

(Bob Larson Collection)

(above) Last, but not least, is classic wood cupola caboose 746, built in 1910. Photographed at Oakland, March 1938.

(Bill Pennington, Bob Larson Collection)

7 WP in the UP System

When Western Pacific was merged into the Union Pacific System in 1985, the company's freight equipment, when repainted, carried the Union Pacific insignia with WP reporting marks. Such painting and lettering adds a new chapter to the WP freight equipment color schemes.

As noted in Chapter 2 on Western Pacific diesel locomotives, one WP GP40 was painted in full UP colors with Western Pacific lettering. The Western Pacific thus became one of six railroads under UP influence to have motive power painted in the UP scheme with individual company sublettering – the others were Chicago & North Western ("Overland Route" passenger power in the 1940s), Milwaukee Road, Southern Pacific (again, passenger motive power), Missouri Pacific; and finally, the RS1s of shortline Spokane International in the early 1950s.

At least one Western Pacific caboose was painted in the full Union Pacific scheme with WP initials. The paint job was quite attractive, and in a way demonstrated a "team" or "partnership" approach.

This chapter illustrates a sampling of WP equipment painted in the UP scheme with WP initials. Even as we roll through the 1990s, the "WP" reporting marks live on.

(facing page) GP40 3532 was the only locomotive to be painted in the UP livery with Western Pacific lettering, before equipment trust legal issues had been resolved. Note the unusual absence of UP lettering in the cab shield.

(Union Pacific Photos)

(right) With the 1985 UP merger, have Western Pacific freight cars disappeared from the scene? Not at all! WP cars began showing up in the mid-1980s with WP reporting marks and UP insignias, such as WP 38110 at Superior, Wisconsin, in September, 1989.

(Author's Collection)

(above) Double plug door, outside post box car 65479 (series 65401-65599) was repainted with WP lettering and a small UP insignia. Council Bluffs, Iowa, December 28, 1988.

(George R. Cockle, Collection of Howard W. Ameling)

(below) WP 65484, now in UP class B170-32, received the full UP livery of boxcar red with white lettering in August 1985. This insulated box car is seen in May 1989 at Council Bluffs.

(George R. Cockle)

Western Pacific covered hopper 11785 (series 11751-11800) with Union Pacific lettering. The car was photographed in a westbound train at Salt Lake City in August 1988.

(Thomas A. Dorin)

WP 11817, on the other hand, carries a newer paint job and a Union Pacific insignia. Council Bluffs, Iowa, March 26, 1989.

(George R. Cockle. Collection of Howard W. Ameling)

Tri-level vehicular flat 89104 (series 89102-89110) is an open-top car in the Union Pacific scheme with the large UP insignia. There were still four such cars on the system roster in 1995. Council Bluffs, Iowa, June 23, 1988.

(George R. Cockle. Collection of Howard W. Ameling)

Western Pacific coiled steel gondolas (series 4401-4425) were classified by UP as G-70-16. Car 4408 was photographed wearing the Union Pacific insignia by George R. Cockle at Council Bluffs, Iowa, on February 25, 1989. There were ten cars of this particular series remaining in 1995.

(Collection of Howard W. Ameling)

Here is Western Pacific 431, part of UP class CA14, painted in the full UP scheme. This paint and lettering application demonstrates what could be called a "partnership" approach to UP's corporate structure. The photo was taken at Council Bluffs, Iowa, in May, 1989.
(George R. Cockle)

Western Pacific (UP) Freight Equipment – 1995

BOX CARS

Series	Outside Length Over Couplers	Capacity	Remarks
3152 - 3167	67-0	134,000	10' door Cushion Frame
3171 - 3178	67-0	173,000	10' door
3219	57-11	148,000	10'6" door
3701 - 3722	69-1	177,000	16' door
3726 - 3736	68-2	163,000	16' door
3737 - 3743	68-5	173,000	16' door
3761 - 3767	68-5	166,000	16' door
3768 - 3775	67-9	169,000	16' door
4059	57-10	141,000	16' door
38002 - 38225	57-3	157,000	16' door
38226 - 38325	56-5	154,000	16' door
39001 - 39009	58-10	145,000	14' plug door
60301 - 60340	57-1	146,000	9' plug door
61051 - 61086	58-0	146,000	16' plug door
62003 - 62048	58-3	141,000	15' plug door Insulated
64003 - 64073	58-2	176,000	15' plug door Insulated
64501 - 64574	57-1	143,000	14' plug door Insulated
64701 - 64748	54-6	135,000	14' plug door Insulated
64805 - 64934	58-10	145,000	14' door Insulated
64955 - 64995	58-3	147,000	14' plug door Insulated

BOX CARS (cont'd)

Series	Outside Length Over Couplers	Capacity	Remarks
65402 - 65599	60-6	137,000	15' plug door Insulated
66001 - 66050	67-9	134,000	15' plug door Insulated
66101 - 66200	69-9	170,000	10' 6" plug door Insulated
66300 - 66348	69-9	169,000	10' 6" door
66501 - 66550	68-11	168,000	15' plug door Insulated
67001 - 67006	68-6	160,000	10' plug door Insulated
67007 - 67018	68-2	162,000	10' 6" plug door Insulated
67020 - 67041	67-10	164,000	10' plug door Insulated
67042 - 67051	68-7	163,000	10' 6" plug door Insulated
67052 - 67054	70-4	168,000	12' plug door Insulated
68228 - 68320	58-2	142,000	10' 6" plug door Insulated
68502 - 68543	58-2	142,000	15' plug door Insulated
68601 - 68766	58-2	143,000	15' plug door Insulated
86002 - 86035	93-9	104,000	20' plug door
86036 - 86102	93-11	142,000	20' plug door

BOX CARS (cont'd)

Series	Outside Length Over Couplers	Capacity	Remarks
86103 - 86127	92-10	148,000	20' plug door

FLAT CARS

Series	Outside Length Over Couplers	Capacity	Remarks
1102 - 1124	90-7	135,000	Containers
1601 - 1602	81-1	300,000	Depressed Center
1811 - 1815	54-1	195,000	
1816 - 1820	54 -1	192,000	
1841 - 1850	64-6	154,000	
1902 - 1906	95-8	122,000	
2109 - 2146	59-3	154,000	
2152 - 2160	64-6	154,000	
2161 - 2167	65-2	154,000	
2169 - 2173	65-2	160,000	
2226 - 2230	59-3	165,000	Depressed Platform
2231 - 2250	56-9	125,000	
2935 - 2963	59-3	120,000	Bulkhead
2994 - 2999	59-3	154,000	Bulkhead
13104 - 13147	64-6	140,000	Bulkhead
13301 - 13316	59-3	115,000	Containers

VEHICULAR FLAT

Series	Outside Length Over Couplers	Capacity	Remarks
89102 - 89110	93-8	73,000	Tri-level auto rack

GONDOLAS

Series	Outside Length Over Couplers	Capacity	Remarks
4401 - 4425	34-6	140,000	Coiled Steel
5101 - 5112	64-11	192,000	Woodchip

GONDOLAS (cont'd)

Series	Outside Length Over Couplers	Capacity	Remarks
6011 - 6015	56-11	175,000	
6201 - 6210	34 -0	200,000	
6308 - 6395	57-7	140,000	
6650 - 6754	57-7	140,000	
6803 - 6843	57-2	162,000	
7701 - 7740	57-1	188,000	

HOPPER CARS

Series	Outside Length Over Couplers	Capacity	Remarks
10048 - 10050	42-3	205,000	Ballast
10201 - 10230	43-9	205,000	
10231 - 10295	44-5	205,000	
10301 - 10575	38-10	200,000	
10604 - 10685	34-3	140,000	Ballast
10701 - 10800	35-1	140,000	Ballast
10801 - 11000	42-10	200,000	

COVERED HOPPERS

Series	Outside Length Over Couplers	Capacity	Remarks
11601 - 11616	42-0	140,000	Airslide™
11617 - 11662	42-1	140,000	Airslide™
11671 - 11685	53-4	188,000	Airslide™
11686 - 11690	53-11	190,000	Airslide™
11691 - 11698	53-4	188,000	Airslide™
11751 - 11800	54-6	196,000	Center Flow™
11801 - 11825	53-10	196,000	Center Flow™
11901 - 11965	54-6	196,000	Center Flow™
11966 - 12000	57-11	197,000	Center Flow™
12001 - 12050	54-6	197,000	Center Flow™
12051 - 12100	57-9	196,000	

Western Pacific covered hopper 11912 (series 11901-11965) with WP reporting marks and Union Pacific lettering.

(Brent MacGregor, Rail Data Services Collection)

WP box car 62033 (series 62003-62048) carries the full Union Pacific yellow scheme.

(Rail Data Services Collection)

8 WP Color Album

(above) The Keddie Wye in winter sees two GP35s and two GP40s in their original paint leading a westbound through freight. Note the black lettering on the trailing unit. March 16, 1969.
(Bob's Photo Collection)

(left) The snow was gone early from Keddie Wye on February 28, 1971, as FP7A 915-D led a GP9 and three more F-units off the "Inside Gateway" line from Bieber, California.
(TLC Collection)

The Burlington Northern merger was about 18 months old on November 12, 1971, but it was already having an impact on pooled BN-Western Pacific motive power consists over the Inside Gateway. In this case, orange and silver WP GP40 3510 leads green BN GP35 2545 and ex-Great Northern "Big Sky Blue" F45 6606 along the Feather River.
(TLC Collection)

Western Pacific F-units added a splash of color to the *California Zephyr's* stainless steel cars, making for a very attractive train. FP7A 805-A, with its winged nose insignia, leads the train through the Feather River Canyon near Pulga, California, on February 12, 1970, about six weeks before the *CZ's* March 22 discontinuance.
(R.R. Wallin Collection)

(above) The first Western Pacific color scheme for the FT units was this incredible green, yellow and red.

(David S. Albrewczynski)

(right) Western Pacific FTs at speed in Utah alongside U.S. 40, on June 27, 1960.

(TLC Collection)

(below) The company's adoption of orange and aluminum for the F-units, as on 910-D at Salt Lake City, created another superb color scheme.

(TLC Collection)

(left) It is New Year's Day, 1971, and this four-unit lash-up at Stockton, California, illustrates three of WP's F-unit color schemes.

(Jim Bruce)

(left) The Perlman green scheme on the F-units is illustrated by F7A 917 at Gait, California, on May 15, 1981.

(TLC Collection)

(below) More WP F-units in action in the Sierra Nevada. F7A 913-D leads a Bieber-bound train up the Inside Gateway out of Keddie on July 29, 1970.

(TLC Collection)

(above) EMD's F-units will go down in history as one of the finest designs in railroading. What better power for a passenger extra than an A-B set of F7s with 914 leading at Keddie, California, on May 23, 1964.

(W. D. Volkmer Collection)

(left) The original WP road switcher color scheme matched the F-units well, as seen on April 4, 1970, with a GP9 and F7B splicing F3 and FP7 cabs recently released from passenger service.

(Tom Brown)

(left) Alco S2 560 in the solid orange scheme at Stockton on October 5, 1975.

(Andy Damonte)

(above) WP SW9 602 in the Perlman green scheme at Stockton on July 28, 1977.
(Mac Owen Collection)

(left) SW9 605 illustrates the later green scheme, with red-orange accents, at Sacramento on May 25, 1981.
(TLC Collection)

(left) SW1500 1503 wears the Perlman green as the WP approaches the "Union Pacific era." Oakland, California, January 23, 1982.
(Jim Bruce)

(left) GP9 731 illustrates the orange and silver application on the early road switchers. At Oakland, California, on July 10, 1977.

(TLC Collection)

(left) The orange and silver eventually gave way to the green scheme, as illustrated by GP9 707 at Salt Lake City in August 1983.

(G. Pekkanen)

(below) WP GP35 3005 in the orange and silver scheme at Sacramento on May 5, 1974.

(TLC Collection)

(above) Four orange and silver U30Bs roll through the Feather River Canyon on February 27, 1970.
(TLC Collection)

(left) GP40 3509 wears the final green scheme, with the addition of red-orange trim, at Salt Lake City on November 8, 1980. The UP power at right is a hint of things to come.
(G. Pekkanen)

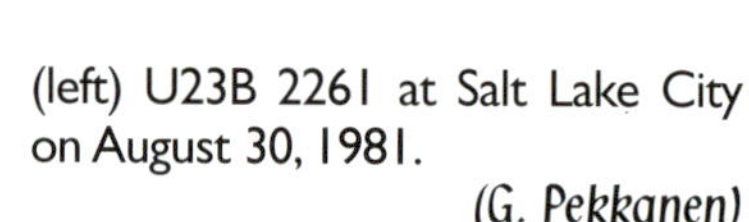

(left) U23B 2261 at Salt Lake City on August 30, 1981.
(G. Pekkanen)

(below) The General Electric U30Bs, like 3064 at Salt Lake City in January 1973, were originally painted in the orange and silver scheme.
(Keith E. Ardinger)

50-foot insulated box car 60040 (series 60001-60050) with "Western Way" script lettering. Equipped with CarPac loader and Shock Control cushioning.
(Rail Data Services Collection)

68-foot outside post plug door box car 67015 (series 67007-67018) in standard red with white lettering. Photographed at San Luis Obispo, California, in June 1983.
(Rail Data Services Collection)

WP 38045 is a 50-foot outside post double door car from series 38001-38225. Photographed at Allentown, Pennsylvania, November 19, 1986.
(Rail Data Services Collection)

(above) Freshly painted WP 60434 (series 60411-60440) is a non-insulated car with a 9' 2" plug door.

(Peter Arnold, Rail Data Services Collection)

Double plug door insulated box car 60747 (series 60651-60800) had a 15-foot door opening, displays the yellow lettering.

(Peter Arnold, Rail Data Services Collection)

50-foot double door car 35056 (series 35001-35099) also had a 15-foot door opening, with "Western Way" lettering in a different style from WP 60040 on the previous page.

(Peter Arnold, Rail Data Services Collection)

(above) 50-foot PS-1 3996 at Oroville (series 3990-3995) was renumbered from WP 36003.

(This page, Peter Arnold, Rail Data Services Collection)

(above right) 68-foot double plug door car 3736 at Stockton (series 3726-3736).

(right) WP 37086 is a 50-foot non-insulated car with a single 10' 6" plug door, part of series 37001-37200.

(below) 50-foot PS-1 in its original orange, black and silver "feather" scheme.

(left) WP 99183 was a typical general service drop-bottom fixed-end gondola, from series 99134-99188.

(Peter Arnold, Rail Data Services Collection)

WP gondolas in the 5001-5070 series were generally used in woodchip service, although freshly-painted WP 5057 was in alfalfa service when photographed.

(Peter Arnold, Rail Data Services Collection)

WP 1890-B was part of a fleet of twin-unit flat cars numbered 1881-1898 A and B.

(Peter Arnold, Rail Data Services Collection)

(left) Flat car 13206 (series 13201-13217) wears the box car red scheme.

(Peter Arnold, Rail Data Services Collection)

(top) Sacramento Northern PS-2 three-bay covered hopper 11538 had reporting marks of parent WP when photographed in September 1964.
(Rail Data Services Collection)

(above) 75893 (series 75801-76232) was one of the stock cars used by WP to serve cattle country.
(Bob's Photo Collection)

(above right) Unit coal train hopper 70018 (series 70000-70240) was among the WP's last new equipment.
(Peter Arnold, Rail Data Services Collection)

(right) Water tank car MW1577.
(Bill Schaumburg, Rail Data Services Collection)

Paint scheme on caboose 429 brought back the old "Feather River Route" insignia.
(TLC Collection)

Bay window caboose 461 mirrors the lettering style used on latter-day WP diesels. Note reflective striping.
(TLC Collection)

Ten roomette-six double bedroom *California Zephyr* sleeper *Silver Range* featured small panels with "WP" ownership lettering. Bedrooms were called "cabins" on the *CZ*.
(Rail Data Services Collection)

Bibliography

Mechanical Records:

Motive Power Diagrams,
Western Pacific Railroad Company.

Freight and Passenger Equipment Diagrams,
Western Pacific Railroad Company.

Work Car Equipment Diagrams,
Western Pacific Railroad Company.

Rosters from Mechanical Records and Listings,
Western Pacific Railroad Company.

Western Pacific Division Timetables:

Eastern Division Timetable 41, July 6, 1947.
Western Division Timetable 35, July 6, 1947.
Eastern Division Timetable 61, April 24, 1960.
Western Division Timetable 46, October 25, 1959.
Consolidated Timetable 1, June 11, 1972.

Railroad Trade Periodicals:

Railway Age, 1943 Volume, Page 610.
Railway Age, May 9, 1955, Page 8.

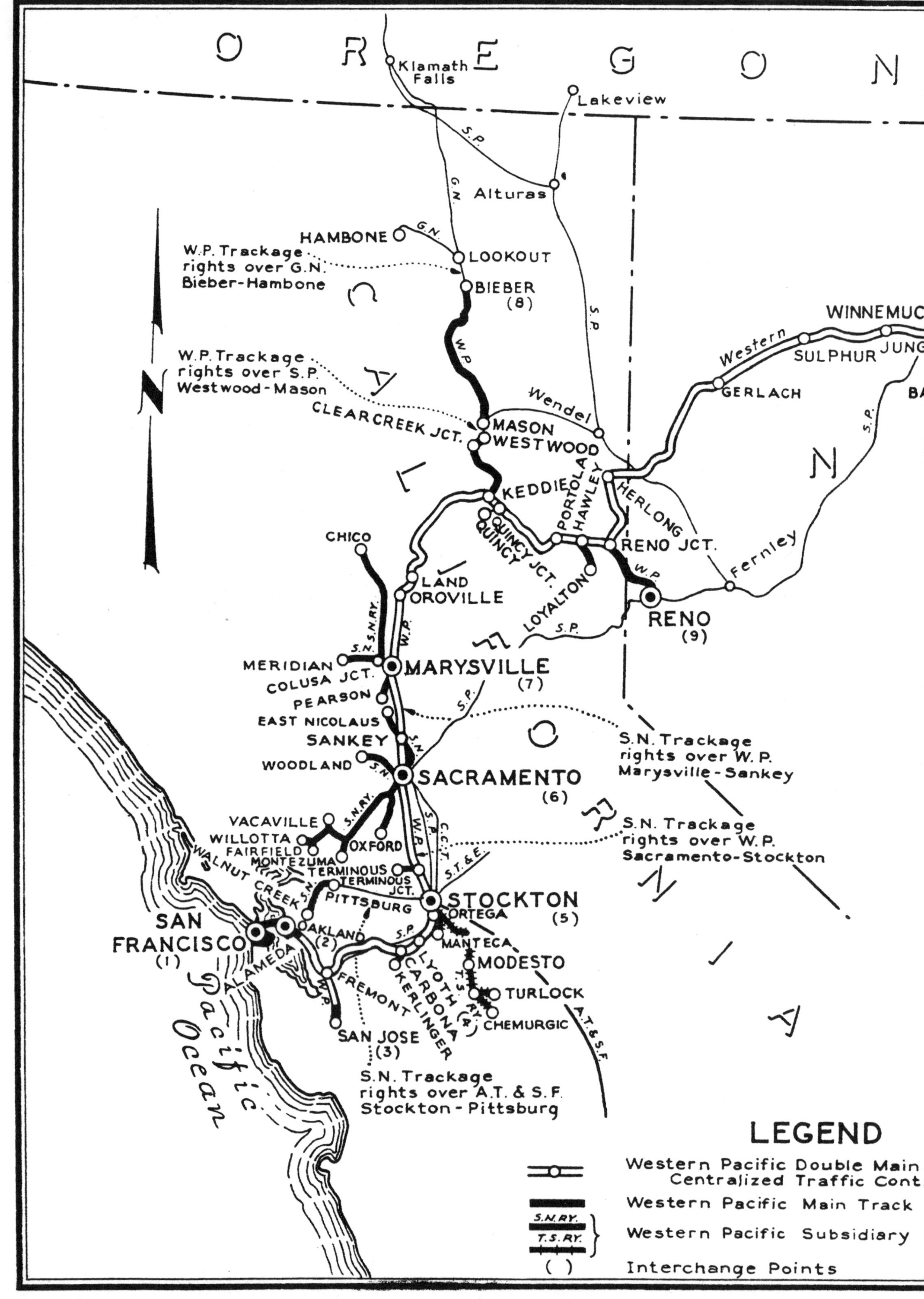
OREGON
Klamath Falls
Lakeview
S.P.
G.N.
Alturas
HAMBONE
LOOKOUT
W.P. Trackage rights over G.N. Bieber-Hambone
BIEBER (8)
W.P.
W.P. Trackage rights over S.P. Westwood-Mason
Wendel
MASON
CLEARCREEK JCT.
WESTWOOD
KEDDIE
PORTOLA
HAWLEY
HERLONG
QUINCY JCT.
QUINCY
RENO JCT.
LOYALTON
WINNEMUC
Western
SULPHUR
JUNG
GERLACH
Fernley
RENO (9)
CHICO
LAND
OROVILLE
S.N.RY.
S.N.
MERIDIAN
MARYSVILLE (7)
COLUSA JCT.
PEARSON
EAST NICOLAUS
SANKEY
WOODLAND
SACRAMENTO (6)
S.N. Trackage rights over W.P. Marysville-Sankey
VACAVILLE
WILLOTTA
FAIRFIELD
MONTEZUMA
OXFORD
TERMINOUS
TERMINOUS JCT.
C.C.T.
S.T.&E.
S.N. Trackage rights over W.P. Sacramento-Stockton
WALNUT CREEK
PITTSBURG
STOCKTON (5)
ORTEGA
SAN FRANCISCO (1)
OAKLAND (2)
ALAMEDA
MANTECA
MODESTO
LYOTH
CARBONA
KERLINGER
FREMONT
T.S.RY.
TURLOCK
CHEMURGIC
(4)
A.T.&S.F.
SAN JOSE (3)
S.N. Trackage rights over A.T. & S.F. Stockton-Pittsburg
Pacific Ocean
CALIFORNIA
NEVADA
N
LEGEND
Western Pacific Double Main
Centralized Traffic Cont
Western Pacific Main Track
S.N.RY.
T.S.RY.
Western Pacific Subsidiary
( )
Interchange Points